# Neuroscience for Organizational Communication

Laura McHale

# Neuroscience for Organizational Communication

A Guide for Communicators and Leaders

Laura McHale
Conduit Consultants Limited
Hong Kong, Hong Kong

ISBN 978-981-16-7036-7     ISBN 978-981-16-7037-4  (eBook)
https://doi.org/10.1007/978-981-16-7037-4

© The Editor(s) (if applicable) and The Author(s), under exclusive license to Springer Nature Singapore Pte Ltd. 2022
This work is subject to copyright. All rights are solely and exclusively licensed by the Publisher, whether the whole or part of the material is concerned, specifically the rights of translation, reprinting, reuse of illustrations, recitation, broadcasting, reproduction on microfilms or in any other physical way, and transmission or information storage and retrieval, electronic adaptation, computer software, or by similar or dissimilar methodology now known or hereafter developed.
The use of general descriptive names, registered names, trademarks, service marks, etc. in this publication does not imply, even in the absence of a specific statement, that such names are exempt from the relevant protective laws and regulations and therefore free for general use.
The publisher, the authors and the editors are safe to assume that the advice and information in this book are believed to be true and accurate at the date of publication. Neither the publisher nor the authors or the editors give a warranty, expressed or implied, with respect to the material contained herein or for any errors or omissions that may have been made. The publisher remains neutral with regard to jurisdictional claims in published maps and institutional affiliations.

This Palgrave Macmillan imprint is published by the registered company Springer Nature Singapore Pte Ltd.
The registered company address is: 152 Beach Road, #21-01/04 Gateway East, Singapore 189721, Singapore

*Every brilliant experiment, like every great work of art, starts with an act of imagination.*

—Jonah Lehrer, *Proust Was a Neuroscientist* (2007)

*The single biggest problem in communication is the illusion that it has taken place.*

—credited to George Bernard Shaw (n.d.)

*For my amazing brother, Captain Anthony McHale of the Ventura County Fire Department, the most gifted communicator I know*

# Acknowledgments

There are many people that I would like to thank for making this book possible:

My remarkable family, who instilled in me the importance of having a rich intellectual life, a love of learning, a big heart, and an even bigger sense of humor.

The extraordinary friends, colleagues, and mentors who unequivocally supported my decision to get a doctorate and encouraged my career continuously in the years since, especially Dr. Mark Gandolfi, Jennifer Quasdorf, Kathryn Hanes, Jennifer Theunissen, Deborah Lee, and Amy Chang.

My former boss, Chi-Won Yoon, for role-modeling leadership so well that he inspired me to study the topic formally.

Dr. Yvonne Ryan for her friendship, unflappable support, and for reading drafts of this book and giving feedback with her exceptional combination of intelligence, wisdom, and kindness.

The many remarkable professors at William James College, from whom I was privileged to learn, especially Drs. Kathryn Stanley, William Hodgetts, Leanne Tortez, Shira Fishman, and Miranda Ralston. Also, my incredible doctoral cohort and fellow students, including Drs. Glenn Sigl, Lisa Mansueto, Stacy Boss, Brandi Derr, Darlene Piva, Jesus Remigio, Omar Bah, and Andrea St. George, among many others.

Dr. Sarah Hill, Tony Melville, and Donata Caira of Dialogix Ltd., whose coaching programs in structural dynamics, generative dialogue, and childhood story changed the arc of my career. Also, to Sarah for generously giving me her time and perspective on publishing a business book.

Giselle Bates—for her friendship, support, and sharp legal insights—and Joe Boschetti, who gave me a very helpful primer on the publishing industry.

Katrina Andrews for her wonderful insights into communications in APAC, business advice, as well as a huge support in increasing my visibility through public speaking opportunities in the region.

Kai-song Ung as well as Sarah Crawshaw for the many rich and enjoyable conversations about communication and organizational psychology, which inspired many parts of this book.

Aruni Nan Futuronsky, and Drs. Stephen Cope and Maria Sirois at the Kripalu Center for Yoga and Health, whose work and wisdom have had an enormous impact on my own.

My incomparable husband, Barry Long, whose friendship, protectiveness, humor, intelligence, playfulness, support, encouragement, and love make everything possible. (And I get my wonderful Kiwi family in the bargain!).

And to you, dear reader. A book is really nothing without anyone to read it. Thank you for picking this one up.

# Introduction

My purpose in writing this book is to show how neuroscience might just be a game-changer for organizational communication. As you will learn in the coming pages, the promise of neuroscience is that it facilitates an unlocking of energy in organizations, tapping into new discoveries about human cognition, emotional regulation, collaboration, and behavior. I believe that using neuroscience to change how we communicate in organizations will help transform them for the better.

I am in a unique position to help translate neuroscience to communicators. Prior to becoming a psychologist, I had a long career in corporate communications and executive speechwriting—mainly working for big European investment banks, in New York, Europe, and most recently in Asia. I enjoyed my career in Comms, and genuinely liked working for big, global organizations with juicy challenges and awesome colleagues. But I had always thought about getting a doctorate, and in 2015, I went back to school to pursue one in the new field of leadership psychology.

My decision to study leadership sprang from a desire to go deeper in terms of understanding what organizational behavior is all about. The catalyst was my work as a speechwriter working for a CEO in Hong Kong. I deeply respected and admired my boss, and I grew curious about how my colleagues, at all levels of the organization, interacted with him. I was also fascinated by how clients and external people interacted with him—nd how those interactions were different. I was surprised by how group behavior changed when he entered a room, and then again when he exited. I noted how people curried favor, attempted (both covertly and not so covertly) to manipulate him, and how a few gravitated toward becoming a strange kind of corporate groupie in his entourage, basking in the glow of his authority. I also noticed, from numerous instances in my own career, how the relationship with a boss could make or break the experience of working for an organization—how great leaders could be immensely inspiring, and how poor leaders could utterly demotivate and dishearten. I noticed how conflicts between leaders impacted morale and created a sense of tribal identity in teams.

I found a remarkable program, that punches well above its weight, at a small school in Boston called William James College. Leadership Psychology is a highly interdisciplinary field. It is not officially recognized as a specialty or subspecialty by the American Psychological Association—though perhaps one day it will be. It is a singular combination of leadership and followership theory, systems theory, adult developmental psychology, coaching psychology, and neuroscience. And it's completely wonderful.

I still remember looking up the program online and feeling my energy shift when I started reading about it. I would love to know what neural pathways were activated at that moment. (Well actually, since I was reading, it started with the visual cortex, which activated the orbitofrontal cortex, which is involved in the cognitive aspects of decision-making. My emotional experience suggests that the amygdala, anterior insula, and ventral occipito-temporal regions were also activated, as these are associated with the sense of intuition (Pillay, 2011). But I digress...). The important thing, in this long story, is that it was in my doctoral program that I discovered one of the great loves of my life, and that is neuroscience.

The neuroscience of leadership (also known as *neuroleadership*) is an interdisciplinary field that explores the neural basis of leadership and management practices (Rock & Ringleb, 2013). Neuroleadership is touted for its ability to use empirically-proven brain research as a basis for understanding and promoting more effective leadership behaviors, particularly for business people, who are more inclined toward "hard" science. I took my first neuroscience class (taught by the amazing Dr. Kathryn Stanley), and it changed the arc of my academic journey as well as my career. I jumped at the chance to be in the first cohort that could choose an area of emphasis in neuroscience. Soon I was dissecting sheep brains and learning about the differences between qEEGs and fMRIs.

My concentration in neuroleadership provided an extraordinary opportunity to survey this emerging field. Neuroleadership is being researched through a variety of lenses, including leadership development (Boyatzis, 2014; Pillay, 2011); human needs and consistency theory (Ghadiri et al., 2014); organizational change (Coe, 2010); behavior change (Berkman, 2018); employee motivation and organizational growth (Swart et al., 2015); decision-making, problem-solving, emotional regulation, collaboration (Ringleb & Rock, 2013); and executive coaching (Habermacher et al., 2014; Boyatzis & Jack, 2018; Pillay, 2011). There is also a growing field studying the cross-cultural applications of neuroscience to organizations, including cross-cultural training (Glazer et al., 2016) and intercultural competency development (McHale, 2019).

But I noticed a gap in the literature when it came to the ever-critical issue of *communication*—not in terms of the individual mechanics of human communication (which has been well studied)—but communication on the organizational and system level, in the corporate, governmental, and non-profit spheres. With this book, I am hoping to remedy that gap and extend the field of enquiry.

This book is not intended to be the definitive guide to the topic, nor does it include any original research. What it does do is synthesize the work of others—phenomenal researchers in neuroscience, neuroleadership, and psychology—and translate them to the practice of organizational communication. Although it is an academic book, I have written it primarily for communications practitioners, organizational leaders, HR specialists, and others who have an interest in communication. I have also written it for graduate students studying communication, psychology, and management. And I hope it will also be of interest to those in the neuroleadership field more broadly.

## References

Berkman, E. T. (2018). The neuroscience of goals and behavior change. *Consulting Psychology Journal: Practice and Research, 70*(1), 28–44.

Boyatzis, R. E. (2014). Possible contributions to leadership and management development from neuroscience. *Academy of Management Learning & Education, 13*, 300–303.

Boyatzis, R. E., & Jack, A. I. (2018). The neuroscience of coaching. *Consulting Psychology Journal: Practice and Research, 70*(1), 28–44.

Ghadiri, A., Habermacher, A., & Peters, T. (2012). *Neuroleadership: A journey through the brain for business leaders.* Springer-Verlag.

Glazer, S., Blok, S., Mrazek, A. J., & Mathis, A. M. (2016). Implications of behavioral and neuroscience research for cross-cultural training. In J. E. Warnick & D. N. Landis (Eds.), *Neuroscience in intercultural contexts* (pp. 171–202). Springer.

Habermacher, A., Ghadiri, A., & Peters, T. (2014, June). The case for basic human needs in coaching: A neuroscientific perspective - The SCOAP coach theory. *The Coaching Psychologist, 10*(1), pp. 7–15.

McHale, L. E. (2019). *The neurocultural leader: Developing self-construal agility for intercultural competency* (Doctoral dissertation). ProQuest Dissertations Publishing. (UMI No. 13863797)

Pillay, S. S. (2011). *Your brain and business: The neuroscience of great leaders.* Pearson Education.

Rock, D., & Ringleb, A. (Eds). (2013). *Handbook of neuroleadership.* Neuroleadership Institute.

Swart, T., Chisholm, K., & Brown, P. (2015). *Neuroscience for leadership: Harnessing the brain gain advantage.* Palgrave Macmillan.

# Contents

| 1 | **From Aristotle to Structural Dynamics** | 1 |
|---|---|---|
|   | *The Neuroscience of Aristotle* | 3 |
|   | *References* | 8 |
| 2 | **The State of Play** | 9 |
|   | *Types of Communicator Roles* | 11 |
|   | *Comms Teams Speak a Different Language* | 13 |
|   | *Shifting Job Titles* | 16 |
|   | *Where Do CCOs Go?* | 17 |
|   | *Changing Technologies* | 20 |
|   |    *AI and Generative Language Models* | 21 |
|   | *Are Comms People Closeted Behavioral Scientists?* | 23 |
|   | *References* | 25 |
| 3 | **The Curious Case of Phineas Gage** | 29 |
|   | *Somatic Marker Hypothesis* | 32 |
|   | *References* | 34 |
| 4 | **Communication in the Brain** | 35 |
|   | *Brain Areas Linked to Speech and Comprehension of Language* | 36 |
|   | *Prosody and Aprosodia* | 37 |
|   |    *Occupational Aprosodia* | 38 |
|   | *The Brain and Social Media* | 40 |
|   |    *The Neuroscience of* Zoom Fatigue | 42 |

|   |   |   |
|---|---|---|
|   | *Some Additional Thoughts on Communication and the Brain* | 44 |
|   | *References* | 44 |
| 5 | **The Body Politic** | 47 |
|   | *Greater Awareness of Office Spaces* | 48 |
|   | *The Importance of the Work Environment* | 49 |
|   | *Changing Office Layouts and Designs* | 51 |
|   | *References* | 52 |
| 6 | **Two Useful Models from Neuroleadership** | 55 |
|   | *The SCARF™ Model* | 56 |
|   | *The SCOAP Model* | 57 |
|   | *Applying the Models to Communication* | 59 |
|   | *Critiques of Neuroleadership Models* | 62 |
|   | *References* | 63 |
| 7 | **The Neurocommunicator's Toolkit** | 65 |
|   | *Meet Your RVLPFC* | 66 |
|   | *The Neuroscience of Stress* | 66 |
|   | *Mindfulness* | 67 |
|   | *Affect Labeling (or Naming Emotions)* | 69 |
|   | *Cognitive Reframing* | 70 |
|   | *The neurocommunicator's Toolkit* | 71 |
|   | *References* | 72 |
| 8 | **The Culture Club: The Neuroscience of Pronouns** | 75 |
|   | *Intercultural Competence* | 76 |
|   | *Cultural Neuroscience* | 76 |
|   | *Self-Construal* | 77 |
|   | *How to Prime Self-Construal* | 78 |
|   | *Why Cultural Neuroscience Matters for Communicators* | 79 |
|   | *Obama's Speech on Race* | 80 |
|   | *References* | 81 |
| 9 | **More on the Neuroscience of Words** | 85 |
|   | *The Politics of Pronouns* | 86 |
|   | *The Nationalist "We"* | 86 |
|   | *Inclusive Versus Exclusive "We"* | 88 |
|   | *The Perils of "I"* | 90 |
|   | *Strong Modals and Weasel Words* | 91 |

| | | |
|---|---|---:|
| | *Text Mining and Sentiment Analysis* | 92 |
| | *The Importance of Clarity* | 93 |
| | *References* | 95 |
| **10** | **The Neuroscience of Compassion** | 97 |
| | *Vicarious Traumatization* | 98 |
| | *Post-Traumatic Organizational Growth* | 100 |
| | *Loss and Grieving* | 101 |
| | *Unlocking Energy* | 102 |
| | *References* | 102 |

**Index**     105

# About the Author

**Dr. Laura McHale (PsyD, CPsychol, ABC)** is a leadership psychologist, lecturer, and author specializing in neuroscience, communication, and organizational culture. She is the founder and Managing Director of Conduit Consultants, a leadership consulting firm based in Hong Kong. Prior to becoming a psychologist, Dr. McHale worked for over 15 years as a corporate communications executive in the financial services industry, across the US, Europe, and Asia. She now spends her time helping leaders and organizations improve communication, increase performance, boost engagement, and build greater stress resilience.

Dr. McHale earned a doctorate (PsyD) in leadership psychology in 2019 from William James College, with a concentration in the neuroscience of leadership. She holds a Master of International Affairs from Columbia University, where she received the *Babsy Marchioness of Winchester Award in Human Rights and Fundamental Freedoms* in 2000. She also holds a Bachelor of Arts in Communication from the University of California San Diego.

Dr. McHale is a member of the American Psychological Association, a Chartered Member of the British Psychological Society, an EMCC Accredited Coach at the Senior Practitioner level, and she holds accreditation in business communication (ABC) from the International Association of Business Communicators.

CHAPTER 1

# From Aristotle to Structural Dynamics

**Abstract** This chapter ties the ancient Aristotelian rhetorical appeals with modern systems theory, specifically David Kantor's theory of *structural dynamics*. We examine a neuroscientific basis for structural dynamics, and how this might be a game-changing framework for communicators to use. We also touch on *neuromania* and the importance of communicators being shrewd and discerning consumers of scientific information.

**Keywords** Aristotelian appeals · Communication domains · Structural dynamics · Neuropsychology

\* \* \*

© The Author(s), under exclusive license to Springer Nature Singapore Pte Ltd. 2022
L. McHale, *Neuroscience for Organizational Communication*, https://doi.org/10.1007/978-981-16-7037-4_1

How we communicate in organizations is perhaps the truest reflection of how we work. It is a barometer of an organization's health. When communication is cautious, inauthentic, propagandistic, or forced, it suggests an organizational culture in distress.

Communications often fail to convey complex organizational realities. This is because the way we approach communication in organizations is fundamentally flawed. Communicators strive for narrative elegance and to reduce complexity in order to communicate more succinctly and economically—especially in today's age of information overload. But in so doing, we tend to sanitize and whitewash differences, rather than enable conversations about them. Moreover, our approach to communication mirrors weaknesses in our approach to management and leadership more generally. This flawed approach to leadership is one of the reasons that so many leadership development programs fail to produce actual leadership skills. As Harvard professor Barbara Kellerman (2012, 2016) pointed out, at least part of the problem is because leadership is a *system*, not a person. If we understand leadership as a system, we realize that we need to develop both individual leaders *and* the human systems they are embedded in. If we understand organizational communication similarly—also as a system—we see new possibilities for what it can enable in terms of dialogue and its ability to stimulate collective intelligence.

But if this is so, how can neuroscience help? How can we use insights about the brain to help us think more systemically about communication?

Organizational theorist Richard Boyatzis (2014) posited that the way MBA programs are taught doesn't make sense from a neuroscience perspective. Research has found that analytical tasks (such as financial analysis, information system engineering, and problem solving), activate regions of the brain known as the task positive network (TPN). However, when a person pays attention to understanding other people, to the emotional realm, to notions of fairness, and openness to new ideas—all critical skills for leaders, by the way—an entirely different network is activated: the default mode network (DMN). The surprising thing is that these two networks have little overlap and actually suppress each other. This presents a significant problem, according to Boyatzis, in that most MBA programs unwittingly focus on skills that activate the TPN (2014).

MBA programs reflect our broader cultural approach to management and leadership. As a result, there is a persistent TPN bias, which has knock-on effects across our organizations, especially for communication. The methods by which we typically communicate in organizations are *implicitly* designed to activate the TPN, and consequently, we are suppressing the DMN. As a result, we constrain our ability to emotionally integrate, build relationships, and develop psychological safety, which stifles our individual as well as collective energy. This book will help explain the process by which this happens, and how we can use neuroscience to remedy it.

## The Neuroscience of Aristotle

Aristotle's three rhetorical appeals—*ethos, logos, and pathos*—have been the building blocks for effective public speaking and communication for millennia. Most corporate communicators use the appeals to craft speeches and presentations. (For more on the Aristotelian appeals, please see *Stanford Encyclopedia of Philosophy*, 2010.)

In basic terms, *ethos* refers to the authority and credibility of the speaker; *logos* refers to the logic or analytic aspects of an argument or appeal, and *pathos* refers to the emotional connection with the audience. In the rhetorical method, all three of the appeals are critical to helping generate interest in and understanding of a topic. It is by neglecting any of the three appeals that communication becomes less effective or fails entirely, either in traditional speeches or even on social media (Nelzén, 2017).

As I delved into psychology, I realized that there were remarkable similarities between the rhetorical appeals and aspects of systems theory, in particular David Kantor's theory of structural dynamics. This insight is especially helpful because it grounds the Aristotelian framework into an empirically proven model. Kantor developed structural dynamics as a model for dialogic practices that enable greater self-awareness, as well as provide a shared vocabulary and framework in which individuals and teams can understand communication (Kantor, 2012). I use structural dynamics extensively in my own consulting practice, to coach individuals and leadership teams that are stuck in non-productive communication patterns, as well as those seeking greater agility in their behavioral repertoire (It's also one of my favorite tools for working with corporate communications teams).

Structural Dynamics has several dimensions (please refer to Kantor's book for detailed descriptions), but one of the most interesting is what Kantor referred to as *communication domains*. These represent the often-invisible "languages" people speak, or areas that individuals tend to focus on during communication. According to the theory, each person usually has a dominant communication propensity within the three domains. This dominant propensity reveals a great deal about what that individual is most likely to pay attention to when they are interacting with others, as well as how they are likely to interact with individuals who are using a different "language." In Structural Dynamics, there are three communication domains: Power, Meaning, and Affect (Kantor, 2012).

Individuals with a higher propensity for Power tend to focus on language around accountability, competence, and getting things done. Individuals higher in the communication domain of Meaning, usually are interested in thinking, logic, and understanding the broader context and overarching purpose. For individuals high in the domain of Affect, they tend to focus on emotional connection and trust (Kantor, 2012). Readers may notice that these three domains are quite similar to the Aristotelian appeals of ethos, logos, and pathos.

*Ethos* refers to the integrity and authority of the speaker—their standing, their qualifications, how they are showing up in terms of their expertise and credibility. This aligns with the domain of Power, and its emphasis on accountability and competence.

*Logos* looks at the logical appeal of an argument, whether it makes sense, corresponds to an established worldview, perspective, or meaning system. This aligns with the communication domain of Meaning, with its emphasis on thinking and logic.

*Pathos* is concerned with emotional appeals to the audience, establishing shared bonds, and building rapport. This aligns with the domain of Affect, with its focus on emotional connection, trust, and caring.

Kantor, just as Aristotle did before him, developed these domains as a framework for describing the underlying, hidden structure of conversations (this structure is the basis of the name "structural dynamics"). Aristotle argued that all three rhetorical appeals needed to be used in effective discourse, and Kantor believed the same. Both understood that a certain rhetorical agility is required and that, to be effective in communication, it is necessary to speak all three languages. People typically have a preference or an overreliance on one domain or appeal over the others, which is sometimes context-specific, but the most effective communicators learn to overcome these limitations and develop proficiency and mastery in them all.

But does neuroscience have anything to say about these communication domains and their related rhetorical appeals?

I believe that it does. The evidence suggests that there may be a neural basis both for Aristotelian rhetoric and structural dynamics. Boyatzis's (2014) research suggests that the TPN and DMN can be activated by different communication domains. For example, the DMN, with its focus on human connection, could be activated by communicating in the domain of Affect. Communicating in power, on the other hand, probably activates the TPN, with its orientation toward achievement and task completion. Meaning, likewise, may also activate the TPN, with its focus on analytic processes and problem solving. However, in structural dynamics, Meaning represents a more expansive construct. Kantor posited that Meaning is also related to openness to new ideas, exploration, and inquiry—which certainly sound like they would activate the DMN. This makes Meaning a more complex domain from a neuroscience perspective (and as such, the evidence from neuroscience may challenge Kantor's premise of Meaning as a single construct, when it may in fact be two: the "analytical" side of Meaning, which activates the TPN, and the "wisdom" side of Meaning, which activates the DMN). We might also see TPN/DMN variations between what Kantor referred to as the *heroic* and *shadow* modes of all three of the communication domains (Kantor, 2012).

If we explore this through systems and leadership perspective, we become curious about what these communication domains look like in the brains of both leaders and followers. The TPN might be activated in followers when a leader is in a heroic Power mode, dazzling with her competence and skill. The DMN might be activated when a leader is in Affect, as he embodies a healthy organizational culture, demonstrates empathy, and learns from mistakes and failures. Meaning may allow a leader to be agile in moving from one neural network to the next, connecting emotions and ideas. But it's important to remember, as Boyatzis (2014) emphasized, that the TPN and DMN suppress each other, so there would be a degree of intentionality in moving from one domain to the other, which is consistent with structural dynamics theory.

There is additional evidence from neuroscience to support an Aristotelian and structural dynamics framework for communication. The psychiatrist and brain researcher Srini Pillay (2011) pointed out that high expertise (e.g., being exposed to an expert, corresponding to *ethos* and Power), not only leads to persuasion, but can lead to long-lasting, enhanced memory formation in the temporal lobe, specifically in the hippocampus. People are, therefore, more likely to better remember what experts tell them versus what laypeople do.

*Pathos*, the realm of emotion and emotional appeal, and Affect also have a compelling neural story. My former professor, Miranda Ralston (2016), researched the specific brain regions and neural correlates associated with resonant and dissonant leadership styles, and their impact on followers' sense of psychological safety. *Pathos*/Affect might also be related to the activation of mirror neurons. These specialized neurons allow individuals and groups to mirror each other's emotions (providing a neural explanation for the "contagion of affect" phenomenon in group relations theory). Research from Goleman and Boyatzis (2008) suggested that mirror neurons are particularly important in organizations, because leaders' emotions and actions prompt followers to mirror those emotions and actions, which activates an array of neural circuits in followers' brains. They argued that the activation of this mirror neural circuitry is a powerful organizational practice and can improve empathy, a sense of shared meaning, cooperation, and connection (Goleman & Boyatzis, 2008).

*Logos* and Meaning may also have a tantalizing basis in neuroscience. The language of Meaning is focused on analytic thought, the archetypal domain of the prefrontal cortex (PFC), and the higher executive functions. However, as we'll discuss in Chapter 2, the Cartesian claim of the clean separation of reason and emotion is more imagined than real (Damasio, 2005)—despite centuries of the Western canon (and most leadership literature) telling us otherwise. From a neuroscience perspective, however, the language of Meaning and *logos* also involves activation of areas of the brain responsible for *cognitive perspective taking*, or what Pillay (2011) described as the ability to "think" what another person feels. This type of perspective taking triggers activation of the ventral medial PFC and creates competitive advantages during negotiation, and in managing difficult conversations (Pillay, 2011).

Given the scope of evidence that suggests a neural basis for Aristotelian rhetoric, as well as Kantor's theory of structural dynamics, I hope readers are now beginning to see the possibilities for our examination of neuroscience for organizational communication.

\* \* \*

This book makes a case for communicators to start thinking about ways they can leverage the incredible knowledge and insights from neuroscience, psychology, and other behavioral sciences to tackle some of the challenges they face. Above all, I hope that this book inspires communicators to up their game.

But I also want to caveat this discussion with the warning that we need to be discerning consumers of neuroscience. One of the reasons that I wrote this book is to try to help separate the wheat from the chaff for communicators. With all the genuine enthusiasm and well-founded admiration for brain science, there is also quite a bit of neuromania and quackery in the air. Andrew Hill, the Management Editor at the *Financial Times*, wryly observed, "Excitement about neuroscience is high. Where it intersects with leadership studies, it is lighting up the prefrontal cortex of coaches, marketers, executives and, inevitably, a few charlatans and snake-oil salesmen" (Hill, 2015). This is an apt observation, and I also have been dismayed by the number of "experts" in neuroleadership who offer coaching and consulting services to organizations and individuals without credentials or formal training in this space.

The same is true of neuropsychology. While Americans have a strict pecking order in professional psychology—only doctoral-level graduates are able to use the moniker "psychologist" (as per the APA definition), and master's-level roles referred to with different terms, such as counselors, specialists, clinicians, etc.,—this is not the case in many countries where only a master's degree is required to use the "psychologist" title. As a result, there are some understandable regional variations on who can call themselves a psychologist.

This disparity becomes problematic, however, in highly dedicated specialties, such as neuropsychology. Given the widespread interest in neuroscience, many coaches, organizational consultants, and psychologists—many with only modest training in neuroscience—are now marketing themselves as "neuropsychologists." Strictly speaking, neuropsychology is a highly specialized field of professional psychology, including *cognitive neuropsychology*, which refers to the study of the structure and function of the brain as it relates to perception and reasoning, and *clinical neuropsychology*, which refers to assessment and rehabilitation from brain injury (American Psychological Association, n.d.). *Neuropsychologists are not, generally speaking, organizational consultants.* Caveat emptor.

# REFERENCES

American Psychological Association. (n.d.). Clinical neuropsychology. In *APA dictionary of psychology*. Retrieved August 22, 2021, from https://dictionary.apa.org/clinical-neuropsychology

American Psychological Association. (n.d.). Cognitive neuropsychology. In *APA dictionary of psychology*. Retrieved August 22, 2021, from https://dictionary.apa.org/cognitive-neuropsychology

Boyatzis, R. E. (2014). Possible contributions to leadership and management development from neuroscience. *Academy of Management Learning & Education, 13*, 300–303.

Damasio, A. R. (2005). *Descartes' error: Emotion, reason, and the human brain*. Penguin Books.

Goleman, D., & Boyatzis, R. (2008). Social intelligence and the biology of leadership. *Harvard Business Review, 86*(9), 74–81.

Hill, A. (2015, April 6). Heads of business need neuroscience. *Financial Times*. https://www.ft.com/content/11812676-d79a-11e4-94b1-00144feab7de

Kantor, D. (2012). *Reading the room: Group dynamics for coaches and leaders*. Jossey-Bass.

Kellerman, B. (2012). *The end of leadership*. HarperCollins.

Kellerman, B. (2016). Leadership—It's a system, not a person! *Daedalus, 145*(3), 83–94.

Nelzén, A. (2017). *Aristotle on social media? Investigating non-profit organizations' usage of persuasive language on Twitter and Facebook*. Bachelor's thesis, Linneuversitetet, Sweden.

Pillay, S. S. (2011). *Your brain and business: The neuroscience of great leaders*. Pearson Education.

Ralston, M. (2016). *A neurological perspective on the effects of resonant and dissonant leadership behaviors on followers and perceived psychological safety*. Doctoral dissertation, ProQuest Dissertations Publishing (UMI No. 10131847).

Stanford Encyclopedia of Philosophy. (2010). *Aristotle's rhetoric*. https://plato.stanford.edu/archives/spr2010/entries/aristotle-rhetoric/

CHAPTER 2

# The State of Play

**Abstract** This chapter reviews the current state of the communications profession. We consider different types of communicator roles, whether communicators speak the same "language" as their colleagues, and why there is a curious lack of lateral mobility of these professionals in organizations. We observe how communicators do not position themselves within a larger behavioral science frame. We also review the potent threats of new technologies, including generative language models such as GPT-3.

**Keywords** Structural dynamics · Generative language models · Behavioral science · Career mobility

\* \* \*

© The Author(s), under exclusive license to Springer Nature Singapore Pte Ltd. 2022
L. McHale, *Neuroscience for Organizational Communication*, https://doi.org/10.1007/978-981-16-7037-4_2

Communication reflects organizational life, which itself mirrors profound transformations taking place in our societies. Organizations are coping with sprawling complexity, information overload, and decreased levels of morale and trust. Technologies that were meant to liberate and connect us have ensnared us. In organizations, we are told to respond to these challenges by being flexible, agile, learn to manage in VUCA (volatile, uncertain, complex, ambiguous) environments, engage in multi-tiered thinking, embrace paradox, develop better work–life balance, work collaboratively, and somehow find enough hours in the day to foster innovation. But all this sometimes feels like magical thinking.

The truth is that many organizations and employees are worn out. And many Comms people are exhausted, after years of having to simultaneously manage all the above, while facing steep learning curves in mastering new technology, performing as an organization's cheerleaders, serving as advisors to senior leaders, keeping a finger on the pulse of the media, and anticipating the evolving needs of clients and employees in an ever-shifting competitive landscape.

Moreover, we have seen some seismic changes in the overall communications landscape. The Covid-19 pandemic has accelerated one of the most dramatic transformations the modern workplace has ever seen. From helping employees and leaders adjust to a global work-from-home experiment, to ensuring business continuity and connection among geographically dispersed stakeholders, the pandemic has delivered unprecedented challenges to the profession. And several of those challenges are here to stay. Flexible working, for many companies, is becoming a permanent feature of organizational life (Jacobs, 2021; Mattu, 2021; Newport, 2021).

It's important to remember that most of these Covid-era challenges accelerated a trend that was already evident: a broader movement toward alternative ways of working and activity-based workplaces. The modern office has seen huge and highly consequential changes in spatial layouts and design. Particularly in many city centers with high commercial real estate costs, there has been a move away from closed offices and cubicles to open-plan environments. These redesigns have often proved controversial with employees, as they have involved significant knock-on effects in terms of lack of privacy, increased noise, and decreased productivity, even as they have been designed to enable greater collaboration (McHale, 2021).

New technology has also brought enormous changes to the communications field. Social media has been around and disrupting the communication landscape for some time (although we are only now learning the extent to which it benefits and threatens our organizations and societies), but new AI-based generative language models, such as GPT-3, are emerging as significant threats to the Communications profession. Generative AI is already well known among journalists, but for some reason it has not yet entered the consciousness of many communications practitioners. As a result, many communicators have a false sense of security, confident in the increasingly erroneous belief that they provide services that could never be outsourced to a machine. Journalists are realizing, and writing about, the fact that GPT-3 can produce credible copy with breathtaking speed and efficiency—and Communications is ripe for the plucking, particularly with so many of our organizational messages being formulaic and uninspired.

But, and at the risk of indulging in an overworn axiom, I also believe that these developments offer communications practitioners an opportunity. Communicators can leverage these technologies to do the more mundane work of comms so that we humans can focus on the higher value-added areas. Only humans can be thoughtful and engaged enough to trigger the mysterious process of motivating employees, clients, and other stakeholders to make better decisions, solve problems more effectively, and bring their full selves to the office. Only humans can foster a sense of openness and curiosity about the plethora of complex emotional experiences we have together—from moments of revelation and deep connection to the psychological injuries, both large and small, that come from work.

Let's explore the state of play.

## TYPES OF COMMUNICATOR ROLES

Communication roles have been traditionally divided into three main areas: *External Communications*, which focuses on media relations and external stakeholders, and usually includes corporate social responsibility (CSR) and executive speeches; *Brand Communications and/or Marketing*, which focuses on an organization's value proposition and brand identity and strategy; and *Internal Communications*, which is sometimes rolled up into an HR department, focusing on employee communication and internally facing executive communication.

Of the three main areas, Internal Comms is the most different animal because of its internal focus, being chiefly preoccupied with employees. Internal comms is best understood as covering the middle part of the larger employee lifecycle, as it picks up from where recruiting/employer brand ends and actual employment begins, and then ceases when employees exit an organization. Former employees, or alumni, then re-enter the external communications world. Because it is internally focused, and therefore not seen as such high stakes, it is the area of Comms that is often the lowest status and as such, it is sometimes under-resourced and under-skilled.

There have always been a lot of gray areas in Communications as a huge array of messages are designed for and applicable to both internal and external audiences. Most communications are not quite binary in terms of audience appeal. This fact accounts for the high degree of role ambiguity within communications teams. Communicators often argue over whose purview a particular message might fall into and this ambiguity reveals both the power dynamics and an internal and external divide that is more fundamental and philosophical than first appears.

In organizational communication, there is always a tension between proactive reputation management and a desire for transparency. The experience of working for an organization is very different than how it is perceived by the outside world. As outsiders, there are things we look for when we are considering joining a new company, and we can sometimes be pushovers for an organization's marketing material and carefully curated brand identity. But when we get inside an organization and see the system from within, the situation changes considerably. The rose-tinting disappears, and reality is brought into relief. And our communication needs change. We need more candor.

External communications practitioners are, at the most basic level, tasked with prevention strategies. They are stewards of the reputation of an organization, as well as the reputation of its senior executives. External communicators learn to be very discerning with how information is communicated. They are naturally cautious, particularly when managing the media. They can be oblique. Media training programs often teach executives (and politicians) to become highly skilled at evasion. This is part of the game that we play in organizations, what organizational consultant Peter Block (2016) described as the *bureaucratic mindset*.

Internal communications practitioners are, at the most basic level, tasked with promotion strategies. The role is essentially about fostering transparency and openness. Internal communicators are tasked with trying to find out what's going on in the organization, enabling two-way communication, and motivating employees to perform better. They try to understand what is on the mind of employees, how to access the intellectual capital employees possess, and how to build a shared sense of purpose.

This creates something of a double bind for the in-house Communications team. Employees smell spin from a mile away and do not appreciate communications that implicitly refute the fact that they are discerning consumers of internal information. Employees have uncanny skills of perception, able to see and feel the gap between an organization's espoused values and its actual in-use culture. Employees especially dislike communications that feel like indoctrination in corporate propaganda, or which contain *marketese* (marketing jargon). Yet, to tell the unvarnished truth—about business conditions, competitive threats, leadership challenges, redundancies, restructurings—isn't so easy, or without consequences especially when the reputation of the company may be threatened, and employees and clients alike are fickle.

So internal communicators often look for ways to hedge their communications, by incorporating a selective degree of authenticity, while being mindful of adverse reputational or legal exposure. Sometimes the result can be a little...vague. I can recall many instances, working in financial services, where I felt like I was getting more information about what was going on in the company from publications such as the *Financial Times* than what was contained in internal emails, town halls, or even conversations with managers. Although external media clearly have their own biases and inaccuracies, incomplete information is usually better than no information at all, especially during a crisis.

## COMMS TEAMS SPEAK A DIFFERENT LANGUAGE

Organizational communicators have a big challenge with language. I am not referring to English, French, Bahasa, or Mandarin, but rather to the aspects of language that we pay most attention to in our organizational lives.

Because internal communicators often need to hedge their bets and navigate the tension between transparency and reputation management, organizational communications tend to seesaw between prevention and promotion strategies. This is probably very taxing for the brain—and for the communicator.

As I discussed in the Introduction, a terrific framework to understand this comes from systems theory, and specifically David Kantor's theory of structural dynamics (Kantor, 2012). One dimension of structural dynamics concerns the three *communication domains* that individuals use when they're interacting. Kantor called these communication domains, which is quite fitting for our purposes here, because they essentially refer to the hidden language that people speak—or more specifically the things that they tend to pay the most attention to while communicating. The three domains are: Power, Meaning, and Affect. Kantor memorably described those who can recognize the hidden structure of communication, and adjust their behavioral repertoire accordingly, as being able to "read the room" (Kantor, 2012).

As a quick review, *Affect* is concerned with the emotional realm, especially in terms of trust and psychological safety within groups, establishing a sense of connection, and a sense of openness and inclusion. The domain of *Meaning* is about analytical thought, big ideas, and an overriding sense of purpose. The domain of *Power* is the most action-oriented of the three communication domains and is focused on shorter-term time horizons, to do lists, and accountability.

In structural dynamics, a frequent cause of conflict, between individuals and in teams, is due to *not speaking the same language*. And sometimes, very often in fact, the *in-use* communication domain of a team or organization is dramatically different from the dominant communication domains of the individuals who comprise that team or organization. This is an especially helpful framework for describing what happens in Communications teams.

While not true in every case, most for-profit organizations communicate in *Power*. It is the language of action, accountability, and completion of tasks. It is the quintessential language of business. Skilled communicators must therefore become fluent in the language of Power if they are going to succeed in these environments. And with many coming from a business journalism background, this usually is not that difficult. Business journalists understand Power.

The problem occurs when organizations are too dominant in one domain. Organizations that communicate in Power, for example, face enormous challenges when they are designing and delivering messages around topics such as organizational culture, leadership development, collaboration, innovation, corporate social responsibility, and other related topics. And leaders, when they try to switch gears to address these topics, often struggle with tone, authenticity, and credibility.

Communicating in Power is not a bad thing, and it's important to remember that there are no "bad languages" in structural dynamics. But it is also important to understand that organizations usually over-rely on one language over the others, and this has an outsized impact on their communication. Note that Power is not the dominant language in every organization: for example, many non-profits are more dominant in the languages of Meaning and sometimes Affect. These companies sometimes need to *practice developing* Power to improve their commercial acumen and ensure that they communicate and interact effectively with business stakeholders.

The overall goal for organizations should be about developing fluency and versatility in all three domains. Different challenges require different languages, as well as different tactics. For communications about organizational culture, for example, we really need to inculcate a sense of trust and psychological safety (Edmondson, 2019). The healthiest organizational cultures are those in which people feel connected, have a shared future, and sense they are safe (Coyle, 2018). Communicators and leaders cannot make those things happen by relying solely on the language of Power. This is where Affect, with its high levels of trust, and Meaning, which rallies toward an overarching purpose and shared vision, can really come in handy.

Let's look at this from a more neuroscientific perspective. Communicating in Power probably activates the task positive network (TPN). However, communicating in Affect would almost certainly activate the default mode network (DMN). Communicating in Meaning probably activates them both; however, not at the same time (remember that each neural network suppresses the other [Boyatzis, 2014]). Meaning, therefore, is an especially interesting language. It enables a movement back and forth from the TPN and DMN. I would surmise that this is the reason that "bystanding in Meaning"—Kantor's term for enabling *generative dialogue*—is such a powerful practice. It allows us to use more of our brains—quite literally.

The in-use communication domain is often a point of concealed tension for teams. More externally oriented communications professionals, who have an implicit preference toward prevention strategies, are often dominant in Power—or if they're not, they learn how to be, but other communicators may struggle with Power. After all, the best communicators are those who can condense complex information into a few core messages and set a fitting emotional tone. This is a skill that requires significant versatility in both Meaning and Affect. This domain clash represents a hidden but taxing dynamic for many teams, and is often a source of tension, both for the team itself but also with other parts of the organization.

It is for these *structural* reasons that organizational communications sometimes come across as a little tone-deaf. Communication rings hollow when it is not delivered in the right language.

I suspect that it is also for these *structural*, rather than *attitudinal*, reasons that many communicators experience such low levels of job satisfaction or find their roles so unsatisfying. The same is probably also true for HR and many other functions that work in the organizational culture space. There is a profound and unmet need for greater levels of Meaning and Affect.

## Shifting Job Titles

Job titles of senior communication roles are beginning to change, no doubt reflecting a broader transformation in the remit of the Communications function. Talking to recruiters, perusing job listings, and gleaning lists of the most influential in-house communicators, such as the *2021 Influence 100* (PRovoke Media, 2021), new patterns are emerging:

- *Head of Corporate Affairs* is increasingly visible as the catch-all title for all activities pertaining to communication and reputation management and is starting to transcend the *Chief Communication Officer* role. Corporate Affairs runs the gamut from internal and external communications to government relations, community affairs, and investor relations. Although the idea of integrating these different functional areas is a compelling story, it will be interesting to see whether one person can really fulfill such a gigantic remit, especially when considering that the information needs of these stakeholders are quite diverse. (I personally am more inclined toward distributed leadership models, such as Heifetz et al.'s [2009] *adaptive leadership*. But this will be an interesting space to watch.)
- Similarly, leaders of internal communication functions are increasingly being referred to as *Head of Employee Engagement*. This is

also a noteworthy development, reflecting a growing awareness that internal stakeholder management involves more than communication, and should be deeply intertwined with an organization's leadership, brand identity, professional development opportunities, and other initiatives pertaining to organizational culture.

The evolution of the types of roles in Communications is worth our study, both as an indication of where the profession is going, but also—and perhaps more importantly—of the challenges that organizations continue to face in the communications space. Clearly there is a need for greater alignment of corporate messages, as the remit of communication gets bigger and bigger. But how does this evolution apply to the career trajectory of communications executives?

## Where Do CCOs Go?

Observers of Chief Communications Officers (CCOs) sometimes note an unusual feature of communications vis-à-vis other infrastructure functions: CCOs tend not to be laterally or upwardly mobile in terms of performing other types of senior organizational roles. In fact, it is extremely rare to hear of a CCO who goes on to become, for example, a Chief of Staff, a COO, or especially a CEO. This is not so true for other infrastructure functions. For example, it's not uncommon to see a Head of HR or a senior Strategy officer move into a Chief of Staff role, or a senior Risk or IT executive, or Head of Business Development become a COO (Bennett & Miles, 2006). And this lack of career mobility is not just about CCOs; it's true for more junior communicators too.

Why would this be the case? Communications executives are trusted advisors to CEOs, and few roles in an organization require as much depth and breadth in terms of understanding an organization's businesses, operations, and political landscape. Communicators are uniquely able to describe and elucidate what makes an organization tick and they have privileged access to the C-suite, where they can peek behind the curtain, see if the emperor has clothes, all the while coordinating and aligning messages. I'm mixing my metaphors here, but it's a valid observation. Communications executives represent a valuable commercial resource, so it's interesting that organizations have not developed better paths for them to become business and operational leaders—and that communicators themselves do not generally aspire to other types of roles (H+K Global, 2020).

Empirical research on this topic is hard to find, but anecdotally, there appears to be one big (and telling) exception to the trend: the political sphere. At least in American politics, as any avid reader of *Politico* knows, it is quite common for communicators working for politicians, particularly politicians in leadership positions, to go on to meaty roles in government or become heads of consulting firms. This is almost certainly because political communicators are positioned to leverage their considerable skills in messaging along with their expert-level understanding of critical issues, and—perhaps most crucially—their access to the levers of power. This provides a singular advantage when positioning oneself as a conduit of information and action. Political communication is intricately interwoven with *strategy*. This is a formidable skill set indeed, but one that somehow doesn't translate to the corporate sphere. In the corporate sphere, Communication is often separated from strategy. The access is there, but not the ability to formulate and change policy.

Indeed, it may be in that very access to the C-suite that corporate communicators are at their strongest and their most vulnerable. CEOs often handpick CCOs and other key Communications staff because these individuals provide personalized messaging and context for a CEO's speaking engagements, as well as a framework for stakeholder management, especially *vis-à-vis* the media. This delicate work requires a high degree of trust. The closeness that is developed means that CCOs are often implicitly seen as one of the CEO's core team, so much so, that in succession scenarios, CCOs are usually caught up in the resulting turnover. In many industries, it is rare for a CCO to remain in place after a CEO transition. New CEOs generally want their own people and are not especially keen to retain members of the *ancien régime*.

This is not the case in politics, where communicators often work for a variety of political leaders, though usually within a particular political party. Again, this may be because communicators in the political realm are regarded more as *strategic advisors* than messaging specialists—and this may not be as true in the corporate sphere.

Another possibility is that perhaps CCOs don't want to go onto other roles. One of the most common career paths into corporate communications, what many CCOs and executives did *before* Comms, is journalism or writing. This isn't all that surprising given that both journalism and

Communications belong to the domain of words, rhetoric, current affairs, and the media. For organizations, it is usually a win to hire individuals tasked with handling the media from media organizations themselves. For journalists, the financial compensation and prestige associated with joining a high-status organization hold enormous appeal (particularly so given the diminishing financial returns of traditional journalism). But after the journalist joins the Comms team, and becomes a spokesperson for an organization, a curious alchemy sets in where they tend to get pigeon-holed into the Comms identity.

I also suspect that this "outsider" status may contribute to a sense of professional inertia. As I mentioned before, it is unusual for communicators to take on other types of roles, either as lateral moves within an organization or in terms of upward mobility, even though such roles tend to foster remarkable personal and professional growth. Sheryl Sandberg, the COO of Facebook, attributed her willingness to try out many different types of organizational roles as a key to developing her own leadership skills and career advancement (Sandberg, 2013). It is good advice, which many communicators do not heed.

Political communicators almost certainly use high levels of Power, Meaning, and Affect, in the structural dynamics sense, in their work. Similarly, the best political speech embodies all three of the Aristotelian appeals. Higher levels of Meaning would also account for the trade-off between financial reward and career fulfillment—many are willing to accept lower pay for greater meaning in their work. The political sphere, of course, sees much lower levels of compensation when compared to the private sector—at least while that individual remains in government. Is a role as a communications advisor to a president or prime minister more meaningful and fulfilling than one for a CEO? It probably depends on the president or the CEO. But what happens after that role is what seems to set communicators apart.

## Changing Technologies

We continue to see technology changing the communications landscape dramatically. Channels of communication, both internally and externally, have grown by leaps and bounds, and social media has completely transformed the external communication strategies of virtually all organizations, both large and small. Organizational and executive communications are subject to the same forces that afflict the internet at large, both beneficial (visibility, voice, direct feedback from customers) and detrimental (disinformation, fake news). Instant interactivity with stakeholders, for better or worse, is now a reality, and communications are transmitted with hyper speed and viral intensity.

The same is not always true with internal communications, particularly in highly regulated industries. Many companies block access to social media platforms for their employees internally. This has led to the development of enterprise social media platforms (ESMPs), such as Yammer, Chatter, and Jive, which allow corporate administrators to enable some degree of interactivity while carefully curating content. While these platforms have not generated comparable levels of engagement and buzz as the better-known external platforms (e.g., Facebook, Twitter), the field has been under-studied, with a surprising lack of peer-reviewed research.

However, this may be changing. A recent flurry of research has demonstrated numerous tangible benefits of ESMPs, including increased employee knowledge sharing (Qi & Chau, 2018), better team improvisation (Sun et al., 2020), and changes to perception management strategies on the part of employees (Sun et al., 2021). It is, however, interesting to note that most of this new research on ESMPs is coming out of mainland China. While this peer-reviewed research is welcome, of high quality, and marks an important contribution to the field, there are concerns about its ecological validity of in settings outside of China. For most mainland Chinese, access to uncensored external social media platforms is highly restricted. It may be the case that ESMPs have more impact in mainland China, and stronger empirical results regarding their efficacy in achieving desirable business outcomes, simply because there are no viable non-enterprise alternatives. More research is needed to know for sure.

## AI and Generative Language Models

There is no doubt that social media has transformed the organizational communications landscape. It has done so primarily through offering a greater range of mediums, but also requiring that messages be adjusted to fit each medium. A classic example is Twitter, where messages need to be condensed to 280 characters. The channel of delivery has an important impact on the context and tone of electronic communications, which I will explore in greater detail in Chapter 4. Marshall McLuhan's famous axiom that "the medium is the message" has never been more relevant (McLuhan, 2013).

Even as social media has changed how organizations communicate, new technologies are transforming the nature of the content itself. AI and *generative language models* are now able to create original content, mimic narrative styles, and in some case, design compelling rhetoric that can sway and motivate. Currently, the most famous generative language model is GPT-3, which was unveiled in 2020 by OpenAI, a San Francisco-based research company.

Those who follow AI know that it is hugely consequential and will have an enormous impact on not only our work lives but on our societies at large, with profound implications for civil liberties, privacy, and governmental regulation. AI technologies cover a sweeping range of possible applications, from facial recognition software to mental health chatbots, to military technology, to the generative language models we are discussing here. Governments and regulators around the world are struggling to catch up to the precipitous pace of technological advancement and implementation. And researchers are also struggling to catch up, to understand the enormous societal impacts these technologies may unleash. In just the past year, we have seen several fascinating studies, with many more in the pipeline. It is a space worth watching and watching closely.

It's clear already that generative AI poses a significant threat to the communications profession. This cannot be overstated. In terms of day-to-day content production such as press releases, corporate announcements, and basic journalism, GPT-3 and its variants can produce convincing and accurate copy in a fraction of the time it takes a human being. The largest, highest-performing GPT-3 variant, DaVinci, even writes jokes (AI Weirdness, 2021). Granted, they are pretty bad jokes, but, if you think about it, so are most people's. The point is that DaVinci can do it.

But don't hand in your resignation slip just yet. We are a long way from being able to surrender organizational communication to a machine, at least for the time being. This is for a few different reasons, and I suspect even more will present themselves in the coming years.

The first reason is that there is a dark side to these technologies. Researchers at Georgetown University found that GPT-3 (terrifyingly) excels at generating disinformation (Buchanan et al., 2021), a phenomenon *Politico*'s AI reporter Melissa Heikkilä (2021) cleverly described as "filling the swamp." The research found that GPT-3 can craft slick and credible-sounding messages with a distinctly partisan tilt, from QAnon conspiracy theories to climate change denial. Other research has shown that generative language models can amplify extremist narratives and radical ideologies (McGuffie & Newhouse, 2020). Just what the world needs…

Most generative AI technologies use something called *reinforcement learning systems*, which adjust themselves to maximize the likelihood that users of these technologies will behave in certain ways. We see this a lot in social media, and there is compelling evidence that reinforcement learning creates powerful feedback loops, which probably is a form of conditioning in that it triggers the brain's reward systems.

While the societal impacts of these developments are for governments and regulators to tackle, it's clear that the rise of the machines to handle more delicate organizational communications will take some time, although perhaps not as much time as we think. It will be interesting to see if and how generative AI, once it is more widely used in the corporate sphere, will mirror the "partisan tilt" of an organization's corporate value proposition, its competitive positioning, and even its own internal systems of political allegiance, privilege, and oppression. I fear we'll find out.

The second reason that generative AI is not coming for your job just yet is that its content is decontextualized. GPT-3 is a generative technology, but it doesn't follow that the content it generates is meaningful or emotionally coherent. It's like Alan Turing's imitation game, where a series of questions can determine if one is interacting with a human or a machine (Turing, 1950). For any issue of real consequence, GTP-3 is an imitation and not the real McCoy.

It is in this sense of imitation that generative AI presents an opportunity for the communications profession. It may liberate communicators from having to produce mundane and humdrum organizational communications and allow them instead to focus on the kind of higher value-added and impactful communications that a generative model would never be able to produce.

And that's where neuroscience and psychology come in. If communicators invest in training in neuroscience and psychology, they will learn to leverage what the research is showing. They can learn to craft messages more in line with how the brain works, humanize organizational communication, as well as position the content they produce in a more meaningful emotional context—something a generative language model will probably (?) never learn to do. Generative AI might just be the push we need to progress the communications profession, by driving communicators to focus on more sophisticated, informed, and sensitive work—that can only be done by people.

## Are Comms People Closeted Behavioral Scientists?

I have a pet theory that many communications and HR practitioners are closeted behavioral scientists. I developed this theory after getting my doctorate, when a surprising number of corporate communications and HR people approached me after hearing me at workshops, watching one of my interviews or podcasts, or via LinkedIn, wanting to get more information and advice about going back to school and possibly becoming psychologists themselves. I believe that this is connected to unmet needs around Meaning and Affect in both the communications and HR professions. In hindsight, that was certainly the case for me.

These discussions helped me realize that I had been a closeted behavioral scientist during my long communications career. Every time I did an employee survey, or conducted a focus group, solicited opinions from leaders, or partnered with HR in engagement initiatives I was doing quantitative and qualitative research. I wish that I knew then what I know now in terms of statistical analysis and survey design, as I would have done $t$-tests and ANOVAs galore, and probably would have managed to get more accurate data than I ever dreamed of having access to at the time.

In behavioral science, we often ask what it is that leads to change? What is it that leads to people making better decisions? What leads to the ability to flourish? And those are questions that communications teams are also tasked with answering by organizational leaders but also among each other as they seek to design impactful programs and strategies.

This is plainly visible at any corporate communications conference. The only difference is that communicators tend to do this work in isolation, without leveraging the training and empirical knowledge of the behavioral sciences.

This is particularly true with internal communications. Leadership teams often bring in the Comms team and task them with getting employees on board with huge change initiatives in order to bring about innovation and better collaboration. Those are really big tasks, and usually almost impossible to deliver. And yet there is a huge field of behavioral science—and emerging field of neuroscience—which strives to provide answers.

Engagement, in particular, is something of the holy grail in organizations and one of the points of richest collaboration between HR, and Communications, and organizational leaders. But what exactly is engagement? It is a quintessential example of a *latent variable*, precisely because it is so difficult to measure. Latent variables are those which cannot be directly observed but rather are approximated through various measures presumed to assess part of the given construct (American Psychological Association, n.d.). There are many ways to describe engagement, and there are differences in engagement pathways for employees versus customers and other external stakeholders. Engagement often includes concepts such as a sense of ownership, a vested stake, loyalty, emotional connection, a sense of belonging, a sense of accountability, a sense of personal investment in the success of a company. So how would we possibly measure these? Well, in behavioral science, we would do it through exploratory and confirmatory factor analysis. Again, it's worth considering why Communicators (and HR practitioners) aren't trained in statistical analysis as a part of their core skill set.

There is a huge case to be made for communicators to get much smarter about how they measure their work, but even before that, how the profession tends to operationalize the variables that they want to measure.

\* \* \*

So, what does it mean to up our game? It means being more expansive in how we understand and define communication, getting curious about what good leadership is, going deeper in understanding the meaning of our work lives, and stretching our skill set in measurement and statistical analysis. It also means being discerning consumers of information and its sources. And even more, it means equipping ourselves as change agents, personally embodying the types of behaviors we want to see in our organizations, and helping workplaces become more humane, kinder, more authentic, and more exciting, motivating, hopeful places to work.

Now, let's dive into the neuroscience!

## REFERENCES

AI writes Star Wars jokes. (2021, May 7). *AI Weirdness.* https://aiweirdness.com/post/650539219288227840/ai-writes-star-wars-jokes

American Psychological Association. (n.d.). Latent variables. In *APA dictionary of psychology.* Retrieved August 22, 2021, from https://dictionary.apa.org/latent-variables

Bennett, N., & Miles, S. A. (2006, May). *Second in command: The misunderstood role of the Chief Operating Officer.* Harvard Business Review. https://hbr.org/2006/05/second-in-command-the-misunderstood-role-of-the-chief-operating-officer

Block, P. (2016). *The empowered manager: Positive political skills at work* (2nd ed.). Wiley.

Boyatzis, R. E. (2014). Possible contributions to leadership and management development from neuroscience. *Academy of Management Learning & Education, 13,* 300–303.

Buchanan, B., Lohn, A., Musser, M., & Sedova, K. (2021, May). *Truth, lies, and automation: How language models could change disinformation.* Center for Security and Emerging Technology. https://cset.georgetown.edu/publication/truth-lies-and-automation/

Coyle, D. (2018). *The culture code: The secrets of highly successful groups.* Bantam Books.

Edmondson, A. C. (2019). *The fearless organization: Creating psychological safety in the workplace for learning, innovation, and growth.* Wiley.

H+K Global. (2020, April 6). *Chief Communications Officers: The new business leaders.* Hill+Knowlton Strategies. https://www.hkstrategies.com/en/chief-communications-officers-the-new-business-leaders/

Heifetz, R. A., Grashow, A., & Linsky, M. (2009). *The practice of adaptive leadership: Tools and tactics for changing your organization and the world.* Harvard Business Press.

Heikkilä, M. (2021, May 26). POLITICO AI: Decoded: Automated disinformation—AI treaty negotiations—Slovenia loves AI. *Politico.* https://www.politico.eu/newsletter/ai-decoded/politico-ai-decoded-automated-disinformation-ai-treaty-negotiations-slovenia-loves-ai/

Jacobs, E. (2021, April 21). The new frontiers of hybrid work take shape. *Financial Times.* https://www.ft.com/content/f568997c-513c-48b0-8422-fabacda46418

Johnston, E., & Olson, L. (2015). *The feeling brain: The biology and psychology of emotions.* Norton.

Kantor, D. (2012). *Reading the room: Group dynamics for coaches and leaders.* Jossey-Bass.

Mattu, R. (2021, July 12). Covid uncertainty means permanent change for managers. *Financial Times.* https://www.ft.com/content/167e7ae7-cd47-46b0-b459-e9ad1a68bfd3

McGuffie, K., & Newhouse, A. (2020). The radicalization risks of GPT-3 and advanced neural language models. *Center on Terrorism, Extremism, and Counterterrorism, Middlebury Institute of International Studies at Monterrey.* https://www.middlebury.edu/institute/sites/www.middlebury.edu.institute/files/2020-09/gpt3-article.pdf

McHale, L. (2021, July 20). *How to help leaders manage the shift to the "new normal" of permanent flexible working.* Conduit Consultants Blog. https://www.conduitconsultants.com/post/how-to-help-leaders-manage-the-shift-to-the-new-normal-of-permanent-flexible-working

McLuhan, M. (2013). *Understanding media: The extensions of man.* The MIT Press (Original work published 1964).

Newport, C. (2021, July 9). How to achieve sustainable remote work. *The New Yorker.* https://www.newyorker.com/culture/cultural-comment/how-to-achieve-sustainable-remote-work

Qi, C., & Chau, P. Y. K. (2018). Will enterprise social networking systems promote knowledge management and organizational learning? *Journal of Organizational Computing and Electronic Commerce, 28*(1), 31–57.

Sandberg, S. (2013). *Lean in: Women, work, and the will to lead.* Knopf.

Sun, Y., Fang, S., & Zhang, Z. (2021). Impression management strategies on enterprise social media platforms: An affordance perspective. *International Journal of Information Management, 60.*

Sun, Y., Wu, L., Chen, R., Lin, K., & Shang, R. A. (2020). Enterprise social software platforms and team improvisation. *International Journal of Electronic Commerce, 24*(3), 366–390.

*The 2021 Influence 100.* (2021, August 2). PRovoke Media. Retrieved August 14, 2021, from https://www.provokemedia.com/research/article/influence-100-provoke-media-reveals-world's-top-in-house-communicators

Turing, A. M. (1950). Computing machinery and intelligence. *Mind, 59*(236), 433–460.

CHAPTER 3

# The Curious Case of Phineas Gage

**Abstract** This chapter examines the brain injury (in 1848) of Phineas Gage, one of the most famous cases in neuroscience. We explore the role of emotional processing in decision-making. We challenge the Cartesian framework, so dominant in leadership, management, and organizational communication. Lastly, we explore the *somatic marker hypothesis* and how it is important for understanding less visible aspects of work.

**Keywords** Decision-making · Emotional processing · Somatic marker hypothesis · Cartesian framework · Phineas Gage

\* \* \*

© The Author(s), under exclusive license to Springer Nature Singapore Pte Ltd. 2022
L. McHale, *Neuroscience for Organizational Communication*,
https://doi.org/10.1007/978-981-16-7037-4_3

In 1848, Phineas Gage, a young railroad foreman in Vermont was involved in a freak and terrible accident that caused a railroad tamping rod to shoot up, at very high speed, under his left eye and exit through the top of his head. Gage survived the accident, and apparently never even lost consciousness, but what happened in the weeks and months that followed became something of an enduring mystery in neuroscience.

The accident was quite gory and caused significant damage to his left eye, cranium, and brain. But astonishingly, after the accident, Gage could speak normally, he retained his memory, and his cognitive functions all appeared normal. His senses were intact, he could remember things and people, and he felt emotions. He could perform motor functions, including complex ones requiring coordination and dexterity. However, Gage's behavior changed, and it changed in a very particular way: he lost his ability to make good decisions (Damasio, 2005; Johnston & Olson, 2015).

The Gage case has become somewhat legendary, though accounts of it vary considerably (Ghadiri et al., 2012; Johnston & Olson, 2015). Based on reports of doctors who chronicled the accident and its aftermath, prior to the accident Gage was relatively unremarkable, lived modestly, and was well-liked in his community. After the accident, however, he started making a series of disastrous decisions. These included curious business choices, imprudent investments, and rumored romantic indiscretions. He became reckless and seemed unable to understand the emotional consequences of his actions (Johnston & Olson, 2015). Doctors at the time were utterly confounded by the case; they knew the behavioral changes were connected to the accident, but they had no way of accounting for the highly selective way that the brain had been injured.

Fast forward to the 1990s, a Portuguese-American neuroscientist, Antonio Damasio (2005), recognized similarities between the Gage case and patients he was working with who had damage to the same parts of the brain as Gage (the ventral medial prefrontal cortex, or vmPFC). Damasio's patients also had intact cognitive abilities and apparently normal functioning of the executive functions of the frontal lobes, but they seemed to lose the ability to do things like generate solutions to ethical dilemmas and they experienced social and financial problems. More succinctly, they seemed unable to understand the consequences of their actions (Damasio, 2005; Johnston & Olson, 2015). This led Damasio to a remarkable insight.

For most of human history, has been generally assumed that decision-making is largely a cognitive function. The frontal lobes, with their awesome powers of reasoning and deduction—unique among animals—were thought to be devoid of emotion. As the esteemed neurologist Elkhonon Goldberg (2009, p. 4) wrote, "The frontal lobes are the most uniquely human of all the brain structures, and they play a critical role in the success or failure of any human endeavor."

For the murkier world of the human psyche, we look to the "emotion centers" of the brain: the amygdala, hippocampus, and limbic system. Emotion was thought to reside exclusively in these areas, and quite separate from what happens in the frontal lobes. However, the story of Gage, and additional cases that Damasio studied, led him to the surprising conclusion that emotional processing and reasoning come together in decision-making.

This was quite a radical proposition. Since Descartes, most of the Western canon has been premised on the presumed separation of reason and emotion. Granted, over the years, many notable artists and philosophers, such as David Hume (1739), refuted the Cartesian framework. But generally, Descartes has had an outsized influence on human affairs, particularly in the fields of economics and business. For example, the archetype of *homo economicus* (economic man), is characterized by the ability to make rational decisions based on rational self-interest (Persky, 1996), one of the foundational principles of modern capitalism.

The danger of this ideal, as the corporate law scholar Lynn Stout (2011) pithily pointed out, is that a true *homo economicus* would probably be classified as a sociopath. *Homo economicus* is, by necessity, cold and calculating, acting out of a "rational" sense of selfishness. According to Stout, this is essentially *antisocial*. More *prosocial* behaviors, on the other hand, are those that enable people to sacrifice their own material welfare when it is in the service of helping, or to avoid harming, others (Stout, 2008, 2011). Prosocial behaviors necessitate emotional connection and empathy—they are also the basis of making society work. Stout (2008) believed that prosocial behaviors could be incentivized to a much greater degree in the judicial system, but also on corporate boards and in corporate and securities law.

This is an important perspective to have. The Cartesian framework represents a persistent bias in the leadership literature, by assuming that leaders are "rational actors," or asserting that leadership consists of a series of measurable traits. Many of us intuitively know that neither is the case, but so frequently in organizations we are asked, for example, to place our trust in leaders or estimate leadership potential. It is only natural that we default to a Cartesian framework of knowing as part of our anxiety management. It is the way that we repress anxiety, both individually and collectively, and maintain an illusion of control.

Of course, this means that *Descartes's error* (a term Damasio coined) is also prevalent in how we communicate in organizations. We communicate as if those drafting the communications—and those receiving them—are primarily rational actors. But Stout's critique of *homo economicus*, combined with Damasio's insights, offer thought-provoking clues as to how communicators can recalibrate this Cartesian bias, to promote more prosocial behaviors in organizations. Since the majority of employees—unlike Phineas Gage—presumably have healthy brains, communicators can do so by providing more emotional context in organizational communications (we'll explore more of how to do that in Chapter 6).

It is important for us to consider Descartes's error because it impacts both *what* we communicate and *how* we communicate it. In organizational life, we tend to have a limited repertoire in terms of the emotions that we "allow" or tacitly encourage. Organizations are like people, and certain emotions are encouraged and rewarded, certain behaviors as well. We want people to be enthusiastic, motivated, authentic, and happy. But we don't seem to have a way of handling when people are unhappy, demoralized, disappointed, or grieving. We need to improve and expand the communication that we use around our emotional experience at work, especially because that experience often involves psychological injury. This doesn't mean that our communications need to become sentimental, gloomy, or like reading an agony aunt column. But it does mean that we can begin to acknowledge the richness of the emotional experience at work, as well as cognitively reframe some of those challenges to help employees process them. This is precisely because emotions provide the optimal activation of the prefrontal cortex (the brain's "accountant") which is critical for decision-making (Pillay, 2011).

## Somatic Marker Hypothesis

There's an additional layer to Damasio's work that I also wanted to mention here. Damasio pointed to the corporeal aspects, the body itself, as instrumental to emotional processing.

The concept of brain–body integration has existed for some time, notably from the early work of the American psychologist William James in the late nineteenth century (for a terrific discussion of James's and other theories, see Johnston & Olson, 2015). Damasio, building on this body of knowledge and partly as a critique of previous approaches, posited the *somatic marker hypothesis* as a new basis for understanding the role of the body in sensing emotion, responding to emotion, and triggering emotion (Johnston & Olson, 2015).

Most commonly, we tend to think of the brain and body connection in terms of emotion preceding its "related" somatic experience. For example, we feel scared and then our heart starts to race, or we feel sadness and we start to cry. The stress cascade has been studied extensively in neuroscience and its sequence is well understood: an external stimulus activates an array of nuclei and systems, including the amygdala, the hippocampus, the anterior cingulate cortex (ACC), the sympathetic nervous system. The ACC is especially fascinating, as it is connected to both the "emotional" limbic system and the "cognitive" prefrontal cortex (Johnston & Olson, 2015; Stevens et al., 2011).

But Damasio's somatic marker says that the reverse is also true: a physical sensation (the marker) can trigger an emotional reaction (Johnston & Olson, 2015).

Have you ever had a physical sensation that triggered an emotional reaction? It may sound counterintuitive, but if you think about it, it happens all the time. It could be something like sensing the sunshine on your face and feeling happy. Having a sore muscle massaged and feeling sad. Sensing a tickle in your throat and feeling dread that you might be coming down with a cold. Putting on your running shoes and feeling a burst of energy.

Neuroscience research, such as Damasio's work, is extraordinary for helping understand the immediacy and interconnectedness of the brain-body connection. And, neuroscience has shown that mindfulness practices can help tease out somatic markers from emotional response (for more on the neuroscience of mindfulness, please see Chapter 6).

Why is this important for organizations and for communicators? Because despite what we know about brain-body interconnection, we tend to completely ignore our bodies at work and in the way we communicate at work.

This needs to change. I'll talk more about the somatic experience of work in Chapter 5. But first, let's go on a tour of the brain and see what communication looks like from a neuroscience perspective.

## REFERENCES

Damasio, A. R. (2005). *Descartes' error: Emotion, reason, and the human brain.* Penguin Books.

Ghadiri, A., Habermacher, A., & Peters, T. (2012). *Neuroleadership: A journey through the brain for business leaders.* Springer-Verlag.

Goldberg, E. (2009). *The new executive brain: Frontal lobes in a complex world.* Oxford University Press.

Hume, D. (1739). *A treatise of human nature.* John Noon. Archived from the original on 12 July 2018. https://web.archive.org/web/20180712120258/http://www.davidhume.org/texts/thn.html

Johnston, E., & Olson, L. (2015). *The feeling brain: The biology and psychology of emotions.* W. W. Norton.

Persky, J. (1996). Retrospectives: The ethology of homo economicus. *The Journal of Economic Perspectives, 9*(2), 221–231.

Pillay, S. S. (2011). *Your brain and business: The neuroscience of great leaders.* Pearson Education.

Stevens, F. L., Hurley, R. A., & Taber, K. H. (2011). Anterior cingulate cortex: Unique role in cognition and emotion. *Journal of Neuropsychiatry and Clinical Neuroscience, 23,* 121–125.

Stout, L. A. (2008). Taking conscience seriously. In P. J. Zak (Ed.), *Moral markets: The critical role of values in the economy* (pp. 157–172). Princeton University Press.

Stout, L. A. (2011). *Cultivating conscience: How good laws make good people.* Princeton University Press.

CHAPTER 4

# Communication in the Brain

**Abstract** In this chapter, we explore neuroanatomy and some of the communication centers in the brain, including Broca's and Wernicke's areas. We consider the concepts of prosody and aprosodia. We introduce the term occupational aprosodia to describe how electronic mediums tend to strip communications of their emotional context. Lastly, we consider the interplay of the brain and social media.

**Keywords** Prosody · Aprosodia · Occupational aprosodia · Language comprehension

## Brain Areas Linked to Speech and Comprehension of Language

There are two main areas in the brain linked to speech: *Wernicke's area* and *Broca's area* (each named for the neurologists who discovered them). In most cases, these areas reside in the left hemisphere of the neocortical brain, but this can vary with handedness: a few left-handed people have Broca's and Wernicke's areas in the right hemisphere. But for most people, they are in the left.

As a quick aside, an important thing to note about the brain is that hemispheric distinctions are enormously complex. In popular culture, it has become quite common to refer to the left hemisphere as the "analytical mind," and the right hemisphere as the domain of "creativity," but this is an oversimplification. That said, there are significant differences between the right and left hemispheres, both structurally and biochemically. For example, spindle cells (thought to be important in human social emotion circuitry) are far more numerous in the right hemisphere than the left, estrogen receptors are more prevalent in the right, and the distribution of neurotransmitters and neuromodulators tends to be asymmetric (Goldberg, 2009).

Wernicke's area and Broca's area are responsible for the production of speech and the comprehension of language. Damage to one of these areas, or both if that were to occur, results in a series of conditions that neurologists call *aphasia*. Wernicke's and Broca's aphasia refers to the inability to comprehend speech or the inability to formulate language (Carlson, 2013). People with Broca's aphasia generally have the ability to comprehend speech, but they have an inability to form grammatically correct sentences. But with Wernicke's aphasia the opposite is true: people are generally able to form grammatically correct sentences but have difficulty comprehending speech (Carlson, 2013).

(One important thing to note in this section is that many of the remarkable things we have learned about the function of the brain's structures are through people who have experienced a traumatic injury, such as strokes or gunshot wounds, or through tumors and other diseases. This should make us very humble. The more we study the brain and its awesome powers, the more we understand how fragile it is.)

Of course, there is a lot more going on in the brain than speech comprehension and formulating grammar when we're engaged in the act of communication (Carlson, 2013). There is an auditory component: the ability to detect and recognize sound, and the ability to interpret those sounds as language. There is also the ability to decipher grammar. The role of memory is critical, including remembering the right words to use and how to say them. And then we have all the motor skills that are involved in moving the face, lips, and tongue. The coordination of the lungs and breathing to utter the sounds. For written communication, there is also the manual coordination and dexterity involved in writing or typing.

But we also have the *co-created* elements of communication, where mirror neurons are activated as people interact. Humans have an astonishing ability to engage in meaningful dialogue. Because of the dialogic nature of communication, a Lacanian framework, with its illumination of the nature of discourse, is helpful to understand that communication is not an individual act that exists in isolation, but rather a co-created system (Bracher, 1994). It is a dynamic process between the person who is initiating the communication and the one who receives it. Furthermore, communication is both an emotional and a biological event. Indeed, much like pain is a subjective feeling of suffering and a physical sensation, communication is a subjective experience as well as a physical and auditory one.

Clearly, there is a great deal happening in communication, and a lot of these processes are taking place in the left hemisphere. There's a whole other marvel going on in the right.

The right hemisphere, in terms of communication, is the part of the brain that is involved with our emotional processing (Carlson, 2013). Recalling the Phineas Gage case and Damasio's work (2005), we know that healthy emotional regulation is critical to the ability to make good decisions. It turns out emotional processing is critical to our communication process more generally.

## Prosody and Aprosodia

One example of this is the concept of *prosody*, which refers to the specific patterns of stress and intonation in spoken language (Carlson, 2013; Esteve-Gibert & Guellai, 2018).

A helpful example of prosody is the phrase: "That's a nice haircut." Whether this statement is a compliment, an insult, or something in between, is down to prosody. The words may be the same, but the intention conveyed through stress and intonation, and with facial expression and body language (many definitions of prosody include these), can change the meaning entirely. The person referencing said haircut might be displaying behavior that is sarcastic and even passive-aggressive, or they may be sincere and kind. (As an aside, it's interesting in English how often the word "nice" means anything but—again, prosody tips us off as to the intention.)

Prosody is often described as is a vocal phenomenon, but there also are visual elements to prosody (Esteve-Gibert & Guellai, 2018). Facial expressions, breathing, and posture are known to induce various emotions, including anger, fear, happiness, and sadness (Laird & Lacasse, 2013). One of the reasons Zoom and other videoconferencing technologies became essential during the Covid-19 pandemic is that they provide prosody—social and emotional context in terms of the ability to see other people's faces and what's going on with their hands. When we look at others on Zoom, we're looking not just for who they are and what they're saying, we're also observing how they're showing up. Are they paying attention? Do they look bored? Do they look engaged? Do they look angry? Neuroscience reveals that humans are, at our essence, incredibly social creatures, and we are constantly monitoring our environments for social threats. Understanding emotional context is therefore critical as we communicate.

### *Occupational Aprosodia*

*Aprosodia* is a neurological condition whereby a person is unable to properly convey or interpret emotional prosody. It is a confounding condition, where an individual can't distinguish between, for example, sarcasm and sincerity (Bateman et al., 2019). Understandably, aprosodia can be a socially devastating deficit to have. As with most emotional processing of communication, aprosodia is caused by injury to the right hemisphere (Carlson, 2013).

But why are we talking about aprosodia in a book about organizational communication? I would argue that one of the key problems we have in organizations is that we unintentionally induce an aprosodic-like syndrome through our organizational communication. I refer to this syndrome as *occupational aprosodia* to distinguish it from the actual clinical disorder. Organizational communication is aprosodic to the degree in which we take communication outside of its emotional context, and this occurs primarily through an overreliance on electronic communications, especially email.

Email is a well-known "frenemy" of the corporate communications profession. It is utterly ubiquitous in organizational life. For years, researchers have studied email and whether it adds to or detracts from effective communication. Researchers have also studied the affective aspects of email communication, particularly because emails tend to inspire very strong, even disproportionate, emotional reactions (Lim & Teo, 2009).

Organizations use email because it is quick, it is cheap, and it can reach a mass audience. Large organizations, in particular, have a dilemma when it comes to leadership access and the geographical, hierarchical, and social barriers which prevent employees, clients, and other stakeholders from interacting with them (Popper, 2013). Manager time is likewise scarce, and resource allocation for face-to-face communication needs to be carefully weighed. Email helps to solve this dilemma by keeping channels of communication open.

However, email has significant downsides. Many of us have observed and experienced a substantial disconnect between what the content of a message is and the emotional context in which it is being delivered (Byron, 2008). This disconnect is critical for communicators to consider, because studies have shown that the use of email has important consequences for employee job satisfaction and organizational commitment (Lim & Teo, 2009). It also has consequences for emotional health. Our ever-increasing overreliance on electronic mediums is contributing to a contextual communication deficit in our organizations—one so serious that it mimics an actual neurological disorder.

Critiques of email and electronic communication are not new, nor are they byproducts of neuroscience research. But understanding what neuroscience reveals about the brain and communication should give communicators and leaders alike cause for concern. The increased use of electronic mediums of communication in organizations has introduced new challenges for employee wellbeing, by powerfully intensifying the pervasiveness of occupational aprosodia. This organizational syndrome has consequences, both in terms of heightened emotional reactivity and also because aprosodia leads to a diminished capacity to understand and interpret more nuanced and subtle communication. Almost 20 years ago, the Yale statistician and graphic artist Edward Tufte (2003) issued his famously blistering critique of the cognitive style of PowerPoint, arguing that it thwarts critical thinking. I would argue that over-reliance on email works the same way: it devolves communication by reducing its complexity and subtlety, and it divorces ideas and data from their emotional context.

The cure for occupational aprosodia is *prosody;* it is allowing that emotional intent to be imbued in the communication. That can best be done, ideally of course, in face-to-face communications, where we can meaningfully interact with one another but there are also a few electronic hacks that are being increasingly adopted by organizations, such as short video clips (Tik Tok style) with organizational leaders, managers, and employees. These quick check-ins are a great idea because they convey prosody, imbuing communications with emotional context that people can immediately relate to.

Videos may not always lend themselves to open-plan work environments (because of noise levels associated with audio), but they can be particularly effective for people in private offices and working from home. Research shows that emojis can also be effective in conveying emotional intent in emails and text messages (Boutet et al., 2021) though they may not be appropriate in a corporate environment or for formal communications.

## The Brain and Social Media

In many cases, however, electronic communications inspire a type of aprosodia, especially with social media (i.e., Facebook and Twitter), whereby the emotional experience of users can become unusually manipulated. Johanssen (2020) demonstrated how social media posts during the Covid-19 pandemic tended to reproduce primitive defense mechanisms (in the Kleinien framework of *paranoid-schizoid* logic), exacerbating fear, denial, and blame. This happens, in Johanssen's view, because social media is explicitly designed to promote particular types of content over others, for purposes of surveillance, advertising, and profit maximization. Other research has pointed to roles of anonymity, invisibility, and particularly lack of eye contact in inducing toxic online disinhibition (Lapidot-Lefler & Barak, 2012).

Official corporate social media posts tend to be heavily vetted, and hence a bit more contained, but they do occasionally go off the rails. In early 2021, Amazon received flak for unusually aggressive corporate tweets directed toward specific American politicians, including

Congressman Mark Pocan, Senator Elizabeth Warren, and others—although this mainly served to highlight the rarity of a corporate voice behaving unrestrainedly and provocatively in the public sphere (Del Ray, 2021).

While examples of terrible press releases and internal email announcements abound (and are usually thoroughly roasted in the media), the truth is that most corporate communications are heavily sanitized and tame. Indeed, the biggest threats to organizations usually do not come from their own social media posts but from external attacks delivered via social media, which can expose companies to significant reputational damage (Amendola, 2019; Brown, 2019).

Even when corporate communications are heavily vetted, the process of vetting itself can be fraught, especially when a groupthink, politicized mentality begins to pervade not just the content but also the construction of the narrative. In a fascinating dissection of the media's handling of the Covid-19 lab leak theory, political blogger Matthew Yglesias explained not only how respected science reporters who had earlier made a case for the lab leak were sidelined but, even more importantly, how a relatively small group of reporters and fact-checkers proclaimed a scientific consensus (around the rejection of the lab leak theory) where none actually existed (Yglesias, 2021).

Yglesias was talking about the media but the same is often true for organizations. Organizational communications tend to promote a narrative of consensus and unity when this seldom reflects the reality on the ground. This is one of the many ways that communication tends to gloss over or minimize difference. It does so is to our detriment because research shows that the minimization of differences stifles the free flow of ideas, dialogue, and discussion that creativity and innovation need to thrive (Hill et al., 2010, 2014). Sanitizing communication makes our organizations less effective, not more.

The lab leak example also highlights an important concept from social psychology known as *self-categorization theory*, whereby people attempt to reduce uncertainty by insisting that their perceptions are "correct." This sense of "being right" is usually reserved exclusively for people who identify as group members (Bordens & Horowitz, 2000; Hogg & Mullin, 1999). Members of the group who have a public voice are bestowed with a disproportionate ability to create these narratives on behalf of the group.

Self-categorization theory is important for communicators to understand because the entire communications function is, in fact, implicitly designed to explicitly create and control organizational narratives. It's the job description you never knew you had.

The common denominator here is uncertainty and it turns out that uncertainty is a powerful trigger of the threat response in the brain, something we will explore in more detail in the next chapter. Modern organizations are highly uncertain places, particularly in industries where technological change is rapid and competitive advantages erode quickly.

It is in these environments that communication has the potential to be transformative. Crafting corporate messages that are sensitive to the fear that comes with uncertainty, where difficult realities are acknowledged, different ways of framing conflict are encouraged, and adaptive responses are co-created can go a long way toward building healthier and more resilient organizations.

### *The Neuroscience of* Zoom Fatigue

With the advent of Covid-19 and the need for so many people to work from home necessitating the widespread use of videoconferencing technologies, the popular press has drawn attention to a phenomenon known as *Zoom fatigue* (Sklar, 2020). While a cognitive or affective syndrome has not yet been identified, the excessive use of videoconferencing is thought to contribute to excessive fatigue. Media coverage of Zoom fatigue usually hypothesizes that videoconferences foster an over-stimulation of the senses: the brain is required to work harder to keep track of so much visual stimuli and its information-processing ability becomes overwhelmed as a result. Because of this, many experts have suggested turning off the video function, or at least using it sparingly during Zoom sessions.

Such advice, while well-intended, it is not consistent with the evidence from neuroscience (McHale, 2020). Research shows that a remarkable percentage of the cerebral cortex is devoted to processing visual information—more than all the other senses combined (Carlson, 2013; Wandell et al., 2007). The hypothesis that videoconferences provide too much visual information to process seems unlikely. In fact, processing visual information is critical to our ability to interpret and respond to a highly complex social environment. We implicitly consider a myriad of social cues whenever we interact, regardless of whether we are online or in person, such as: who is present, how they are showing up, what their mood is, and where their gaze is directed (Leopold & Krauzlis, 2020).

Furthermore, as we learned in our discussion of prosody, much of the ability to construe emotional intent is not just conveyed through tone of voice and word choice, but also by means of somatic movements produced by the hands, head, and especially the face (Esteve-Gibert & Guellai, 2018). Relinquishing the ability to detect these visual cues might itself cause anxiety and lead to more fatigue, rather than the other way around.

It is much more likely that the fatigue associated with Zoom and other videoconferencing platforms has more to do with users' *affective states* than the neuroscience of visual processing. It has to do with how we feel about being "on camera" for long periods of time. The subjective experience of being visible to others can change depending on our emotional context and mood—how we are showing up on a particular day. Sometimes we very much want to be seen; other times we do not. The inclination toward "invisibility" probably has both adaptive and maladaptive aspects, but some of it appears to be related to a fundamental need for privacy.

In organizational life, there are times we would prefer not to be seen. Zoom may be fatiguing because sometimes it intrudes into our privacy, especially when we are working from our own homes. In that sense, Zoom fatigue is probably more about *surveillance* than it is about visual processing.

One strategy I recommend for videoconferencing is to disable the self-face view. Neuroscience has shown that humans, when given the option, seem to be hard-wired to focus on their own faces rather than the faces of other people (Ma & Han, 2010; Sui et al., 2009, 2013). The reasons for this interest in our own faces are not well understood, but it is thought to be a critical component of self-awareness (Han, 2017). In an interesting aside, the effect is more pronounced in left-handed people, who have an advantage in self-face recognition due to their higher levels of right prefrontal activity (Keenan et al., 2000).

A big problem with Zoom is that it provides, via the video interface, a constant mirror of the self-face (unless the self-view is manually hidden by the user). When the self-view is enabled, the result is an involuntary focus on how the visual self appears. This is not how we usually have meetings or conversations in person. Having our eyes drawn to our own faces is not an indication of vanity or narcissism but rather it reflects the wiring of the human brain and its inherent preoccupation with the self—a dynamic the technology accidentally stumbles into.

Because of all of this, I recommend that the self-view be hidden, whenever it is appropriate to do so, simply because it is distracting and thwarts the ability to focus on the faces of those we are communicating with. This is especially helpful in one-to-one meetings on Zoom. Just don't forget that you are still on camera! One important exception to this advice is when giving presentations to large audiences, where it is usually not possible to see audience members while in screen-sharing mode. In these cases, using the self-face view is both helpful and reassuring to ensure you are visible to others.

### *Some Additional Thoughts on Communication and the Brain*

The neurologist Elkhonon Goldberg (2009) argues that the distinction between diseases of the brain and diseases of the soul is becoming increasingly blurred. Our magnificent frontal lobes, which enable us to engage in all sorts of luminously advanced functions, including the powerful emotional aspects of communication, are also responsible for some of our most profound vulnerabilities. This chapter has highlighted some of the mechanisms in which some of those vulnerabilities manifest, especially in terms of how we communicate with one another at work.

But one of the key learnings from neuroscience is the concept of *neuroplasticity:* the mechanism by which neural pathways change in response to experience or environment (American Psychological Association, n.d.). Our brains are always changing, always adapting, always responding to our environment in the moment. But our brains like to plan. The very existence of neuroplasticity gives us cause for optimism because it suggests that human cognition is much more about the future than the past. Through imagination and language—and the very act of communication—we create models of both the things that do not yet exist and the things we hope to create (Lehrer, 2007; Goldberg, 2009).

## REFERENCES

Amendola, J. (2019, August 9). How social media can make or break your business's reputation. *Forbes.* https://www.forbes.com/sites/forbesagencycouncil/2019/08/09/how-social-media-can-make-or-break-your-businesss-reputation

American Psychological Association. (n.d.). Neuroplasticity. In *APA dictionary of psychology*. Retrieved August 22, 2021, from https://dictionary.apa.org/neural-plasticity

Bateman, J. R., Filley, C. M., Ross, E. D., Bettcher, B. M., Hubbard, H. I., Babiak, M., & Pressman, P. S. (2019). Aprosodia and prosoplegia with right frontal neurodegeneration. *Neurocase, 25*(5), 187–194.

Bordens, K. S., & Horowitz, I. A. (2000). *Social psychology* (pp. 316-354). Lawrence Erlbaum.

Bracher, M. (1994). On the psychological and social functions of language: Lacan's theory of the four discourses. In M. Bracher (Ed.), *Lacanian theory of discourse: Subject, structure and society* (pp. 107–128). New York University Press.

Brown, J. (2019, July 9). How social media could ruin your business. *BBC*. https://www.bbc.com/news/business-48871456

Byron, K. (2008). Carrying too heavy a load? The communication and miscommunication of emotion by email. *Academy of Management Review, 33*(2), 309–327.

Carlson, N. R. (2013). *Physiology of behavior* (11th ed.). Pearson.

Damasio, A. R. (2005). *Descartes' error: Emotion, reason, and the human brain*. Penguin Books.

Del Ray, J. (2021, March 28). Amazon started a Twitter war because Jeff Bezos was pissed. *Recode*. https://www.vox.com/recode/2021/3/28/22354604/amazon-twitter-bernie-sanders-jeff-bezos-union-alabama-elizabeth-warren

Esteve-Gibert, N., & Guellaï, B. (2018). Prosody in the auditory and visual domains: A developmental perspective. *Frontiers in Psychology, 9*, 338.

Goldberg, E. (2009). *The new executive brain: Frontal lobes in a complex world*. Oxford University Press.

Han, S. (2017). *The sociocultural brain*. Oxford University Press.

Hill, L. A., Travaglini, M., Brandeau, G., & Stecker, E. (2010). Unlocking the slices of genius in your organization: Leading for innovation. In N. Nohria & R. Khurana (Eds.), *Handbook of leadership theory and practice: An HBS centennial colloquium on advancing leadership* (pp. 611–654). Harvard Business Press.

Hill, L. A., Brandeau, G., Truelove, E., & Lineback, K. (2014). The inescapable paradox of managing creativity. *Harvard Business Review*. https://hbr.org/2014/12/the-inescapable-paradox-of-managing-creativity

Hogg, M. A., & Mullin, B.-A. (1999). Joining groups to reduce uncertainty: Subjective uncertainty reduction and group identification. In D. Abrams & M. A. Hogg (Eds.), *Social identity and social cognition* (pp. 249–279). Blackwell.

Johanssen, J. (2020). Social media and coronavirus: Paranoid-schizoid technology and pandemic? *Human Arenas*. https://doi.org/10.1007/s42087-020-00162-2

Keenan, J. P., Wheeler, M. A., Gallup, G. G., Jr., & Pascual-Leone, A. (2000). Self-recognition and the right prefrontal cortex. *Trends in Cognitive Science,* 4(9), 338–344.

Lapidot-Lefler, N., & Barak, A. (2012). Effects of anonymity, invisibility, and lack of eye contact on toxic online disinhibition. *Computers in Human Behavior,* 28(2), 434–443.

Laird, J. D., & Lacasse, K. (2013). Bodily influences on emotional feelings: Accumulating evidence and extensions of William James's theory of emotion. *Emotion Review,* 6(1), 27–34.

Lehrer, J. (2007). *Proust was a neuroscientist.* Houghton Mifflin Company.

Leopold, D. A., & Krauzlis, R. J. (2020, February). How the brain pays attention to others' attention *Proceedings of the National Academy of Sciences,* 117(8), 3901–3903.

Lim, V. K. G., & Teo, T. S. H. (2009). Mind your E-manners: Impact of cyber incivility on employees' work attitude and behavior. *Information & Management,* 46, 419–425.

Ma, Y., & Han, S. (2010). Why we respond faster to the self than to others? An implicit positive association theory of self-advantage during implicit face recognition. *Journal of Experimental Psychology: Human Perception and Performance,* 36(3), 619.

McHale, L. (2020, June 9). Three tips for reducing "Zoom fatigue," based on neuroscience. *Conduit Consultants Blog.* https://www.conduitconsultants.com/post/three-tips-for-reducing-zoom-fatigue-based-on-neuroscience

Popper, M. (2013). Leaders perceived as distant and close: Some implications for psychological theory on leadership. *The Leadership Quarterly,* 24, 1–8.

Sklar, J. (2020, April 24). 'Zoom fatigue' is taxing the brain. Here's why that happens. *National Geographic.* https://www.nationalgeographic.com/science/2020/04/coronavirus-zoom-fatigue-is-taxing-the-brain-here-is-why-that-happens/

Sui, J., Liu, C. H., & Han, S. (2009). Cultural difference in neural mechanisms of self-recognition. *Social Neuroscience,* 4, 402–411.

Sui, J., Hong, Y., Liu, C. H., Humphreys, G. W., & Han, S. (2013). Dynamic cultural modulation of neural responses to one's own and friend's faces. *Social Cognitive and Affective Neuroscience,* 8(3), 326–332.

Tufte, E. R. (2003). *The cognitive style of PowerPoint.* Graphics Press.

Wandell, B. A., Dumoulin, S. O., & Brewer, A. A. (2007). Visual field maps in human cortex. *Neuron,* 56, 366–383.

Yglesias, M. (2021, May 26). The media's lab leak fiasco: A huge fuckup, with perhaps not-so-huge policy stakes. *Slow Boring.* https://www.slowboring.com/p/the-medias-lab-leak-fiasco

CHAPTER 5

# The Body Politic

**Abstract** This chapter explores the somatic experience of work. We discuss how and why communicators can play a much more powerful role in workplace redesign strategy. We consider research into the environmental aspects of office life, including natural light, green plants, and artwork. We also investigate *interoception* and *proprioception* and the importance of movement.

**Keywords** Interoception · Proprioception · Workplace redesign · Natural light

\* \* \*

© The Author(s), under exclusive license to Springer Nature Singapore Pte Ltd. 2022
L. McHale, *Neuroscience for Organizational Communication*, https://doi.org/10.1007/978-981-16-7037-4_5

One of the most overlooked aspects of what happens at work is what takes place with our bodies. The somatic components of work are critically important because, as we saw in the last chapter, what happens in the body is inextricably and indispensably interwoven with the brain. Yet too often in organizations, and our resulting communications, when we talk about work, we tend to only talk about mental output. It's as if only our brains come to work and not our bodies.

The title of this chapter is a play on words, referencing both the traditional metaphor of how governments and institutions are conceived of as a body (Britannica, n.d.), but also in the feminist theory sense of *body politics*, or the practices and policies of social groups, organizations, and governments which ensure that bodies conform to socially and politically accepted constructions and norms (Brown & Gershon, 2017).

Through this lens, it becomes apparent how organizations exert enormous influence over what happens to our bodies while we are working, from what we wear and how our bodies are adorned to how we occupy physical space and the degree to which our somatic freedom is enabled or restricted. But perhaps the most essential way is how we interact with our work environment.

## Greater Awareness of Office Spaces

Communicators tend to be relentlessly focused on the lauded (and usually quite privileged) areas of organizations, such as the C-suite and high-performing individuals, teams, and businesses. This can sometimes lead to neglect in developing closer collaborations with infrastructure teams, who exert a subtler but powerful influence on organizational life. A good example is corporate real estate departments, which usually have wide sway over the ways our offices are set up and the spatial arrangements we work within.

For many communicators, partnering with these teams is not considered very high-status work. Office moves and/or transitions to open plan environments are often disruptive and unpopular with employees and can be a significant drain on the resources of busy communications teams. In fact, it is not uncommon for large organizations to outsource communication to design firms and other external consultants. This is usually a self-defeating strategy, however, because beneficial outcomes are increased when organizations allow employees themselves to have a say in a process (Knight & Haslam, 2010).

Rather than being tasked with communicating after the critical decisions have been made, communicators who are informed about the brain/body aspects of work are in a better position to serve as advisors to project teams that work on office redesign. Communicators have insight into the downstream impacts of organizational initiatives, they are well-equipped to articulate the overall goals of projects and skilled at parsing out strategies based on those goals. They particularly excel at identifying different types of audiences and stakeholders, anticipating what the communication needs of those groups are, as well as the likely structural and attitudinal barriers to implementation. This can be an invaluable source of perspective for project teams, and one that should be tapped into much earlier in the process.

## *The Importance of the Work Environment*

An environment that allows people to perform their work under comfortable conditions is a fundamental human requirement (Roelofsen, 2002). There is substantial empirical evidence that environmental conditions contribute powerfully to the employee experience.

Most office workers compete for desk locations with a view. Access to these rarefied spaces tends to increase with seniority and as individuals advance up the corporate hierarchy, up to and including landing the proverbial (and actual) corner office. The desire for a room with a view is often assumed to be related to a human need for aesthetic beauty, as well as status. While these are no doubt true, research shows that access to natural light has a profound impact on the brain. Natural light has been shown to significantly influence mood, stress, and sleep quality, and office workers who sit closer to windows report significantly better outcomes in these areas (Figueiro et al., 2017; Shishegar & Boubekri, 2016). Natural light is an important type of *zeitgeber*, or external and environmental cue that synchronizes a person's biological rhythms (Carlson, 2013).

Green plants have also been shown to have remarkable positive benefits on office workers, including increases in job satisfaction (Dravigne et al., 2008), as well as anxiety and stress reduction, enhanced memory retention, increased creativity, and enhanced productivity and attention (Hall & Knuth, 2019).

Office artwork has also been shown to have a positive impact on employee behavior and mood. Art can promote social interactions, elicit emotional responses, boost imagination, and enhance the subjective experience of work (Smiraglia, 2014). Some organizations showcase the art in their offices just like a museum would, complete with expert curators on staff, which can be a remarkable way to impress clients as well as enhance the employer's value proposition. But artwork in the office does not need to be grand to be impactful. Even modest attempts to bring in artwork can yield impressive results.

Another important aspect of organizational environment is the degree to which people can physically move around. There is no doubt that movement should be promoted more at work, particularly for knowledge workers. The detrimental effects of sitting at a desk all day have been studied for some time and these risks have been compounded by the Covid-19 pandemic to a significant degree. Encouraging breaks and recommending that people go for walks are surprisingly powerful practices for helping employees improve emotional regulation and boost creativity (Pillay, 2011).

There is a growing body of research on what is known as *embodiment*, and the sub-field of *embodied cognition* specifically explores how postures and bodily movements influence emotional states and stimulate thinking and insight (Pillay, 2011; Veenstra et al., 2017). This concept is, of course, intricately woven into Damasio's somatic marker hypothesis (Damasio, 2005).

What occurs at work in terms of embodied cognition reflects larger societal trends. Many aspects of modern life, including desk work, the use of technology, and the masking of symptoms with medication, have reduced what is known as *interoception,* or the ability to detect internal sensations such as pain, hunger, and thirst (Plans, 2019). Disrupted interoception appears to play a key role in many mental health conditions, including anxiety and mood disorders, eating disorders, and addiction (Plans, 2019), and almost certainly reduces workers' effectiveness. Despite this, research into the role of interoception in the workplace is surprisingly rare but it is a promising field of inquiry. For example, a recent study in Japan showed that workers with higher interoceptive awareness demonstrated higher work performance (Tanaka et al., 2021).

Fatigue, so pervasive in modern organizational life, has been shown to reduce *proprioception*, or conscious awareness of the body's movements (Yung, 2016). This also has striking workplace ramifications. Knowledge workers often lose their sense of proprioception because of the sedentary nature of sitting at a desk all day. Reduced proprioception, or kinesthesia, can lead to an impaired sense of one's own body position, diminishing the awareness of somatic experience, and increasing the likelihood of injury.

Some organizations have responded to the risks of sedentary work by introducing new office furniture options, such as adjustable-height desks and workstations. Research shows that such interventions can have positive benefits for employee health (Shrestha et al., 2015). These include improved cardiovascular outcomes and reduced pain and discomfort while working (Chambers et al., 2019). Unfortunately research has also shown that only about half of employees who have adjustable-height workstations use them regularly (Wallman-Sperlich et al., 2017). Wallman-Sperlich et al., (2017) found that the failure to use these workstations, in many cases, was due to resistance around employers' efforts to regulate employee behavior in the workplace—a finding that foreshadowed, four years later, similar tensions related to mask-wearing and vaccination mandates during the Covid-19 pandemic. The evidence suggests—for communicators and leaders—that workplace wellness initiatives may be more complex than they appear, and require well-thought-out and strategic communication plans.

## *Changing Office Layouts and Designs*

Although Covid-19 brought office life to a standstill, in many ways the pandemic merely accelerated a trend that had already been evident: the move toward alternative ways of working. Particularly in cities with high commercial real estate costs (e.g., Hong Kong, New York, London), office layouts have been increasingly moving away from private offices and cubicles to open plan environments and/or hot-desking and working from home. Many office redesigns have proven controversial with employees, as they involve significant knock-on effects in terms of lack of privacy, increased noise, and decreased productivity, even as people are able to collaborate more (Congdon et al., 2014; Hoendervanger et al., 2016; Palvalin & Vuolle, 2016).

Prior to the pandemic, high-quality, peer-reviewed research on these new workplaces was still a bit esoteric, with a few studies published in corporate real estate journals and only occasionally appearing in mainstream business publications.

The research raised more than a few red flags in terms of how office redesigns impacted individuals and teams but usually also shared several strategies and approaches that could mitigate the risks. What was surprising to me, as an organizational consultant working on communication strategies related to office redesign at that time, was how little senior leaders were aware of—or cared about—what the research revealed, primarily because the cost-savings of such projects proved irresistible.

The Covid-19 pandemic changed the calculus completely. The new office reality, for many workers, now looks likely to include at least some degree of permanent flexible working, and employees are more likely to be spending a much greater percentage of their time outside the traditional office (Jacobs, 2021; Newport, 2021).

Working from home may offer better opportunities to incorporate practices that enable greater interoception, proprioception, and the chance to go outside and interact with nature. We can hope. There is a risk, however, that working from home may increase the sedentary aspects of knowledge work, as well as exacerbate the already diminished quality of social connections with peers and colleagues. Much of this may be down to the choices individuals make, in terms of how they choose to work and engage with each other, but it will also be down to the messages sent by senior leaders. This is an area where communicators can play an important role.

\* \* \*

As this chapter has shown, the relationship of our work environment to our somatic experience is a critical component of how we show up. As Winston Churchill famously observed, "We shape our buildings; thereafter they shape us" (Churchill, 1943).

## REFERENCES

Brown, N., & Gershon, S. A. (2017). Body politics. *Politics, Groups, and Identities, 5*(1), 1–3.

Britannica. (n.d.). Body politic. In Encyclopedia Britannica online. Retrieved August 22, 2021, from https://www.britannica.com/topic/body-politic

Carlson, N. R. (2013). *Physiology of behavior* (11th ed.). Pearson.

Chambers, A. J., Robertson, M. M., & Baker, N. A. (2019). The effect of sit-stand desks on office worker behavioral and health outcomes: A scoping review. *Applied Ergonomics, 78*, 37–53.

Congdon, C., Flynn, D., & Redman, M., (2014, October). Balancing "we" and "me": The best collaborative spaces also support solitude. *Harvard Business Review*. https://hbr.org/2014/10/balancing-we-and-me-the-best-collaborative-spaces-also-support-solitude

Churchill, W. (1943, October 28). *House of commons rebuilding* [Speech transcript]. Hansard 1803–2005. https://api.parliament.uk/historic-hansard/commons/1943/oct/28/house-of-commons-rebuilding

Damasio, A. R. (2005). *Descartes' error: Emotion, reason, and the human brain*. Penguin Books.

Dravigne, A., Waliczek, T. M., Lineberger, R. D., & Zajicek, J. M. (2008). The effects of live plants and window views of green spaces on employee perceptions of job satisfaction. *HortScience, 43*, 183–187.

Figueiro, M. G., Steverson, B., Heerwagen, J., Kampschroer, K., Hunter, C. M., Gonzales, K., ... Rea, M. S. (2017). The impact of daytime light exposures on sleep and mood in office workers. *Sleep Health, 3*, 204–215.

Hall, C., & Knuth, M. (2019). An update of the literature supporting the well-being benefits of plants: A review of the emotional and mental health benefits of plants. *Journal of Environmental Horticulture, 37*, 30–142.

Hoendervanger, J. G., De Been, I., Van Yperen, N. W., Mobach, M. P., & Albers, C. J. (2016). Flexibility in use: Switching behavior and satisfaction activity based work environments. *Journal of Corporate Real Estate, 18*(1), 48–62.

Jacobs, E. (2021, April 21). The new frontiers of hybrid work take shape. *The Financial Times*. https://www.ft.com/content/f568997c-513c-48b0-8422-fabacda46418

Knight, C., & Haslam, S. A. (2010). The relative merits of lean, enriched, and empowered offices: An experimental examination of the impact of workspace management strategies on well-being and productivity. *Journal of Experimental Psychology: Applied, 16*(2), 158–172.

Newport, C. (2021, July 9). How to achieve sustainable remote work. *The New Yorker*. https://www.newyorker.com/culture/cultural-comment/how-to-achieve-sustainable-remote-work

Palvalin, M., & Vuolle, M. (2016). Methods for identifying and measuring the performance impacts of work environment changes. *Journal of Corporate Real Estate, 19*(3), 164–179.

Pillay, S. S. (2011). *Your brain and business: The neuroscience of great leaders*. Pearson Education.

Plans, D. (2019, 5 February). We've lost touch with our bodies: But we can get it back through a process known as "interoception." *Scientific American*. Available at: https://blogs.scientificamerican.com/observations/weve-lost-touch-with-our-bodies/

Roelofsen, P. (2002). The impact of office environments on employee performance: The design of the workplace as a strategy for productivity enhancement. *Journal of Facilities Management, 1*(3), 247–264.

Shrestha, N., Ijaz, S., Kukkonen-Harjula, K. T., Kumar, S., & Nwankwo, C. P. (2015). Workplace interventions for reducing sitting at work. *Cochrane Database of Systematic Reviews, 1,* CD010912.

Shishegar, N., & Boubekri, M. (2016, April 18–19). Natural light and productivity: Analyzing the impacts of daylighting on students' and workers' health and alertness. In *Proceedings of the International Conference on "Health, Biological and Life Science"* (HBLS-16), Istanbul, Turkey.

Smiraglia, C. (2014). Artworks at work: The impacts of workplace art. *Journal of Workplace Learning, 26*(5), 284–295.

Tanaka, C., Wakaizumi, K., Kosugi S., et al. (2021). Association of work performance and interoceptive awareness of 'body trusting' in an occupational setting: a cross-sectional study. *BMJ Open, 11.*

Veenstra, L., Schneider, I. K., & Koole, S. L. (2017). Embodied mood regulation: The impact of body posture on mood recovery, negative thoughts, and mood-congruent recall. *Cognition and Emotion, 31*(7), 1361–1376.

Wallmann-Sperlich, B., Bipp, T., Bucksch, J., et al. (2017). Who uses height-adjustable desks? –Sociodemographic, health-related, and psycho-social variables of regular users. *International Journal of Behavioral Nutrition and Physical Activity, 14*(26).

Yung, M. (2016). *Fatigue at the workplace: Measurement and temporal development.* PhD Dissertation. University of Waterloo. https://uwspace.uwaterloo.ca/handle/10012/10119

CHAPTER 6

# Two Useful Models from Neuroleadership

**Abstract** This chapter introduces two models from the neuroscience of leadership (or neuroleadership) that are especially useful for communicators. The SCARF™ model reveals the primary threat and reward triggers in the brain, and the SCOAP model looks more holistically at human needs. The chapter also includes examples of how each may be applied to organizational communication. Lastly, we explore some of the potential pitfalls of neuroleadership approaches.

**Keywords** SCARF model · SCOAP model · Neuroleadership

\* \* \*

© The Author(s), under exclusive license to Springer Nature Singapore Pte Ltd. 2022
L. McHale, *Neuroscience for Organizational Communication*, https://doi.org/10.1007/978-981-16-7037-4_6

As I explained in the Introduction, the neuroscience of leadership (also known as *neuroleadership*) is an interdisciplinary field that examines leadership and management through the lens of brain science. The chief advantage of this approach is that it provides an empirically validated basis for what are often considered to be the "softer" behaviors and attitudes involved in leadership.

As a reminder, neuroleadership has been researched through a variety of lenses, ranging from leadership development and organizational growth to collaboration and intercultural competency development (please refer to the Introduction for a more comprehensive list). Each approach is fascinating in its own right. However, for our purposes here, there are two neuroleadership models that stand out. Each provides a thoughtful frame for understanding how communications can be more effective from a neuroscientific perspective. In this chapter, we will explore them in detail.

## The SCARF™ Model

The first model, David Rock's SCARF™, is the more well known (Rock, 2008; Rock & Ringleb, 2013). With its straightforward acronym and approach, the SCARF™ model is very elegant and easy to remember—something of a rarity in the neuroscience literature.

The components of SCARF™ are Status, Certainty, Autonomy, Relatedness, and Fairness. SCARF™ is best understood as a framework for the primary reward and stress triggers in the brain, and, more specifically, the ones that we are most likely to experience in a work context. These are incredibly helpful to know about from a communications perspective because communicators and leaders alike often unwittingly tread on these triggers and initiate stress reactions in people without realizing it.

In the SCARF™ methodology in a nutshell, Status refers to our importance relative to others; Certainty is the ability to predict the future; Autonomy is our ability to exert control over events; Relatedness is our sense of connection; and Fairness is the fair exchange between people (Rock, 2008).

Most of these concepts are known stress triggers from our own subjective experience, but Rock's work has demonstrated that there is a compelling body of research that reveals that each type of event triggers profound, and often unique, changes in the brain. One of the most striking is Relatedness, which is closely connected to the idea of social inclusion or exclusion. It turns out that social exclusion is an uncommonly painful event; it lights up virtually all the pain centers of the brain, much the same way that a physical injury would (Cacioppo & Cacioppo, 2016). As such, Relatedness has huge ramifications for diversity and inclusion in organizations.

Fairness is another fascinating one. Research reveals that humans are not alone in being intensely focused on issues of fairness. Experiments show that other primate species will not perform tasks or participate in games if they are obviously rigged or perceived to be unfair (Brosnan, 2013). This suggests that fairness may have evolved as a survival strategy and core part of the social system formation in primates.

It's clear that the SCARF™ model offers some very intriguing perspectives, and I'll share suggestions for applying it to communications a little later in this chapter. But first, let's explore the second neuroleadership model that I recommend for organizational communicators.

## THE SCOAP MODEL

The second model is lesser known but packs a punch in terms of the rich psychological theory it is drawn from, as well as its applicability to organizational communication. It is Ghadiri et al.'s SCOAP model (2012).

The SCOAP model is based on the work of the late German psychologist Klaus Grawe and his theory of human needs, known as *consistency theory* (Ghadiri et al., 2012). Consistency theory involves positioning human needs in the context of the larger environment. This makes it a very dynamic, systems-based approach, which holistically incorporates the role of followers in the leadership equation (something sometimes missing from neuroleadership research). In consistency theory, humans are believed to have a fundamental set of basic needs, and when these needs are not adequately met it leads to impairments in mental health and well-being.

SCOAP components each represent a different human need: Self-esteem, Control, Orientation, Attachment, and Pleasure. According to the model, each of these needs has a different expression in leadership (Ghadiri et al., 2012).

While SCARF™ excels at understanding the threat and reward triggers in the brain that we're most likely to encounter in an organizational setting, the SCOAP model provides a deeper perspective in terms of what motivates human behavior more broadly.

Ghadiri et al. (2012) adapted Grawe's work by identifying the specific neural correlates and circuits that correspond to each need. They modified Grawe's theory in one important way: they parsed out the difference between control and orientation (which Grawe had considered to be different aspects of the same need), because neuroscience showed that control and orientation each triggered different neural events.

While most of the needs in the SCOAP model are self-explanatory, it is worth spending a little time exploring them further. One of the most interesting needs, because it does not often pop up in the leadership literature, is the need for Attachment. This was first identified in the seminal work of John Bowlby (1951) and refers to the ways in which people feel secure, avoidant, ambivalent or disorganized in terms of their how they form connections with others. This is the need that is most related to leader–follower interactions, especially because humans tend to project childhood experiences of authority onto leaders, often without conscious awareness (Fraher, 2004; Myburg, 2009).

Attachment is partly related to the concept of Relatedness in the SCARF™ model, although attachment looks more at the nature of the relationship with others rather than just the affective experience of the individual. We know from SCARF™ that the sense of Relatedness is critical in the brain. With the SCOAP model, Ghadiri et al. explored the neural aspects of relatedness and the sense of attachment, including the role of oxytocin as the "bonding" or trust hormone, which has since been studied to a greater degree in work environments, particularly in teams with high psychological safety and trust (Zak, 2014).

The needs for Orientation and Control are really about the ability for individuals to design and develop their own environment (Ghadiri et al., 2012). This sense of Control is highly related to Certainty in the SCARF™ model, as is the need for Orientation. Orientation is threatened when goals are unclear, or information is ambiguous. This is particularly relevant to organizations coping with rapid technological change. Organizations with VUCA (volatile, uncertain, complex, ambiguous) environments pose some of the biggest challenges around the need for Orientation and Control.

The need for Self-esteem is different from the other needs because it is tied not only to a sense of social connection but also to a sense of the inherent worth of the self. This sense of self-worth, according to

Habermacher et al. (2014) is only made possible by the ability to be introspective and reflective. They believe that self-esteem is difficult to research at a neuroscientific level and indeed, I would agree that it is a very difficult variable to operationalize. Part of the reason may be due to self-esteem being a problematic construct. In a thought-provoking article, Crocker and Park (2004) argued that measures of self-esteem as being high or low may be less important than understanding the narrow domains in which self-esteem is often pursued. They also challenged the conventional wisdom that self-esteem is a universal attribute, when in fact it may be a culturally-contingent construct. This fascinating argument might shed light onto why this need is so difficult to measure.

The last human need as outlined in the SCOAP model is Pleasure. Pleasure is about feelings of reward and positivity. The neuroscience of reward is very complex, and we are still learning about fascinating differences in reward, such as the differences between liking, wanting, and learning (e.g., Berridge's work as cited in Johnston & Olson, 2015). The inclusion of Pleasure is refreshing because Pleasure is not commonly referred to in the organizational literature, although it clearly is an unsung preoccupation in much of our work lives. In the SCOAP framework, Pleasure is not only concerned with the avoidance of pain but how it is profoundly tied to the limbic system, which is thought to be the center of hedonic reward.

The SCOAP model is much more complex than my description here, and I encourage readers to read the book and journal articles for a more complete summary (including their fascinating discussion of approach and avoidance schemata for each of the SCOAP needs). But what is central here, in our discussion of communication, is how SCOAP provides a more informed awareness of human well-being.

Now let's look at applying these models with some concrete examples of what it might look like.

## Applying the Models to Communication

What are the key takeaways from SCARF™ and SCOAP? Well, the first one is that neuroscience offers fascinating insights into leadership more generally. Another key takeaway is understanding that humans, at work or anywhere else, are primarily emotional beings. And the third is that we have an empirically validated set of human needs and specific triggers of the threat/reward response.

So how would we go about applying these insights to organizational communication?

Let's begin with SCARF™ and framing its components as activating the reward systems in the brain. Examples of effective SCARF™-centric messages might include (and I'll focus on internal communications here):

*Status*: Your work forms a critical part of this organization's success
*Certainty*: The one thing we know for sure is that this change is coming, and we need to be prepared for it
*Autonomy*: We encourage you to manage this process in accordance with your own needs and preferences
*Relatedness*: Your presence is an asset to this team
*Fairness*: We realized this organizational change wouldn't be meaningless unless it applied to everyone

Okay, so you get the general idea. Consciously incorporating SCARF™ principles supports the reward network and can help frame communications in a more humane light. *One major caveat, however, is that these words are meaningless unless the organizational culture actually backs them up.*

So, let's take a turn with messages that might trigger the threat response in the brain. Some of these may sound eerily familiar and indeed, now that you know what to look for, you may notice these types of messages everywhere. Our organizations are riddled with them. Pay attention to the discomfort, that heady combination of anxiety and cynicism that arises when we are being forced to drink the corporate Kool-Aid, because that feeling tips off that the threat response has been activated, which is causing measurable changes in your brain and somatic functioning—exactly the kind we are learning to avoid. Hone that awareness as a guide to help you to design better communications.

Here are some examples:

*Status*: Meetings will be held with senior managers: all other employees will be communicated with in due course
*Certainty*: At this time, it is not possible to make contingency plans
*Autonomy*: Effective immediately, all employees are required to…

*Relatedness*: The [all white male] senior management team believes diversity is a priority and business imperative
*Fairness*: This policy will apply to all junior employees; however senior managers will be exempted.

The fascinating thing about all the examples above is that it would probably be possible to reframe each of them into something that is less likely to trigger the threat. For the "effective immediately" types of announcements, the threat can be mitigated by providing context, being forthcoming about the circumstances behind certain decisions, or describing the larger organizational context. And some of these statements will depend on if the audience is a *beneficiary* or a *target* of the message. For example: "Meetings will be held for senior managers: all other employees will be communicated with in due course" will lift the status of senior managers (a reward), while reducing that of junior employees (a threat). Many organizational communications are double-edged in this way, which is why smaller, more targeted communications are often necessary.

Just as we did for SCARF™, let's now take a look at how we might use the SCOAP model to craft better communications. Unlike SCARF™, the SCOAP model looks more holistically at the human experience, and in particular the area of human needs.

Here are some examples of some possible SCOAP-centric messages based around human needs:

*Self-esteem*: This exemplary work highlights the best of what our people can achieve
*Control*: "We will give you the tools and support you need to navigate this change successfully
*Orientation*: These seismic changes, of course, are not just impacting our company, but the industry as a whole
*Attachment*: Employees like you, who demonstrate such grit and determination, will always have a home here
*Pleasure*: There is a time for hard work and a time for rejuvenation. Now is the time for the latter. May we all enjoy this well-deserved holiday.

Although there are endless variations in terms of how messages can incorporate either SCARF™ or SCOAP principles, I hope it is clear is that both are useful for designing communications that are more attentive to human needs and avoiding the well-known triggers of stress.

## CRITIQUES OF NEUROLEADERSHIP MODELS

While these models have much to offer the practice of organizational communication, there are several concerns or potential pitfalls with both models and the field of neuroleadership more generally.

The first concern is that neuroleadership tends to oversimplify the construct of *leadership*. Leadership is extraordinarily complex and, in the words of Barbara Kellerman (2016) at Harvard, is best understood as a *system* not a person. At the very least, leadership is a co-created process between leaders and followers. After all, without followers there is no leadership. Yet, followers are curiously, and consistently, neglected in the neuroleadership literature. So is systems theory more generally.

Secondly, one cannot really talk about leadership without understanding the context in which it takes place. For that, you must account for environmental factors, the nature of the organizational culture in which leaders find themselves embedded, and also issues pertaining to racial/cultural identity as well as gender. Once again, these are extraordinarily complex to tease out.

Thirdly, neuroleadership research presents some thorny challenges for statistical analysis and validity. This is partly because of the difficulty in operationalizing these complex leadership variables for empirical study, and many neuroleadership studies (and those pertaining to the neuroscience of management more broadly), rely on rather overly simplistic measures and scales. It is also because the brain imaging technology involved in neuroscience research is notoriously expensive, and therefore sample sizes for experiments tend to be quite low. These factors contribute to concerns in terms of the construct validity of experiments and whether there is sufficient power for statistical analysis in small samples of larger populations.

Fourthly, many neuroleadership approaches feature a heavy reliance on *trait theory*, reducing leadership to a series of measurable attitudes, beliefs, and behaviors. Neuroleadership could benefit from applying additional theories of human personality (e.g., psychodynamic, humanistic, and adult developmental models), as well as more deeply exploring the complex relationship between personality and behavior.

And lastly, there is also a tendency, in at least some of the literature, to link leadership behaviors exclusively to the brain's threat and reward functions. This is problematic for a few different reasons. One reason is that each of these systems is immensely complex, and each activates different parts of the brain. For example, there are numerous brain systems that mediate reward (the ventral striatum and nucleus accumbens in the midbrain for starters), but reward is also powerfully mediated by the neurotransmitter *dopamine*, and there are dopamine receptors in the anterior cingulate cortex as well as the prefrontal cortex, which are completely different parts of the brain (Johnson & Olson, 2015). For the threat response, we see the activation of the amygdala and the hypothalamic–pituitary–adrenal axis for starters, as well as the release of *norepinephrine*, another powerful neurotransmitter, but this happens not just in the brain but throughout the body. Can neuroleadership studies really measure activities in all these systems when examining leadership behaviors?

The threat/reward approach may also be too limited a window through which to frame leadership. There's more to us than seeking pleasure and avoiding pain. Leadership is not just about motivating performance with carrots or sticks. Leadership is also about fostering *eudaimonic wellbeing*, or the sense of contentment that is achieved through having a meaningful purpose at work and in life (American Psychological Association, n.d.; Klenke, 2007). Eudaimonically oriented leaders often display characteristics such as hopefulness, optimism, and resilience (Klenke, 2007). Given that such aspects of psychological safety have been linked to positive outcomes at both the individual and organizational levels (Luthans et al., 2010), we need more neuroleadership studies that focus on these areas.

For these reasons, psychology and systems theory can offer many rich spaces for future collaboration in the neuro leadership field. This will be an exciting space to watch.

## References

American Psychological Association. (n.d.). Eudaimonic well-being. In *APA dictionary of psychology*. Retrieved August 22, 2021, https://dictionary.apa.org/eudaimonic-well-being

Bowlby, J. (1951). *Maternal care and mental health*. World Health Organization.

Brosnan, S. (2013, June). Justice and fairness in nonhuman primates. *Proceedings of the National Academy of Sciences, 110* (Supplement 2), 10416–10423.

Cacioppo, S., & Cacioppo, J. T. (2016). Research in social neuroscience: How perceived social isolation, ostracism, and romantic rejection affect our brain. In P. Riva & J. Eck (Eds.), *Social exclusion* (pp. 73–88). Springer.

Crocker, J., & Park, L. E. (2004). The costly pursuit of self-esteem. *Psychological Bulletin, 130*(3), 392–414.

Fraher, A. L. (2004). Systems psychodynamics: The formative years of an interdisciplinary field at the Tavistock Institute. *History of Psychology, 7*(1), 65–84.

Ghadiri, A., Habermacher, A., & Peters, T. (2012). *Neuroleadership: A journey through the brain for business leaders*. Springer-Verlag.

Habermacher, A., Ghadiri, A. & Peters, T. (2014, June). The case for basic human needs in coaching: A neuroscientific perspective—The SCOAP coach theory. *The Coaching Psychologist, 10*(1), 7–15.

Johnston, E., & Olson, L. (2015). *The feeling brain: The biology and psychology of emotions*. W.W. Norton & Company.

Kellerman, B. (2016). Leadership—It's a system, not a person! *Daedalus, 145*(3), 83–94.

Klenke, K. (2007). Authentic leadership: A self, leader, and spiritual identity perspective. *International Journal of Leadership Studies, 3*(1). http://www.regent.edu/acad/global/publications/ijls/new/vol3iss1/klenke/klenke.htm

Luthans, F., Avey, J. B., Avolio, B. J., & Peterson, S. J. (2010). The development and resulting performance impact of positive psychological capital. *Human Resource Development Quarterly, 21*, 41–67.

Myburg, H. (2009). *The experience of organisational development consultants working in the systems psychodynamic stance*. http://uir.unisa.ac.za/handle/10500/1473.

Rock, D. (2008). SCARF: A brain based model for collaborating with and influencing others. *NeuroLeadership Journal, 1*, 44–52.

Rock, D., & Ringleb, A. (Eds). (2013). *Handbook of neuroleadership*. Neuroleadership Institute.

Zak, P. (2014). The neuroscience of trust. *HR People & Strategy, 37*(1), 14–17.

CHAPTER 7

# The Neurocommunicator's Toolkit

**Abstract** This chapter introduces the right ventral lateral prefrontal cortex (RVLPFC), considered to be the brain's "braking system." We explore the neuroscience of stress, and three interventions from neuroscience that can activate the RVLPFC and interrupt the stress cascade:

© The Author(s), under exclusive license to Springer Nature Singapore Pte Ltd. 2022
L. McHale, *Neuroscience for Organizational Communication*,
https://doi.org/10.1007/978-981-16-7037-4_7

mindfulness, affect labeling, and cognitive reframing. We discuss how to apply these interventions to organizational communication.

**Keywords** RVLPFC (right ventral lateral prefrontal cortex) · Stress · Mindfulness · Affect labeling · Cognitive reframing

## Meet Your RVLPFC

One of the most fascinating parts of the brain is an area known as the right ventral lateral prefrontal cortex or RVLPFC. Thanks primarily to the work of Matthew Lieberman (2009) at UCLA, the right RVLPFC burst onto the scene as a region of significant interest because it appears to be involved in just about every type of self-control that we have. From not eating that second doughnut to managing to bite your tongue in response to some provocation, everything that keeps you focused, on-task, and emotionally nimble is connected to it. It's your RVLPFC you can thank in those lovely moments when you are able to take a deep breath and not be subjected to intense emotional reactivity, even when things get stressful.

In the brain, self-control manifests in a variety of ways (Lieberman, 2009). For example, there's *motor* self-control, which is what helps keep you from driving on the wrong side of the road in a foreign country. There is also *cognitive* self-control, which allows you to keep your concentration and focus (e.g., I need to finish this thought but I really want to make my morning cup of coffee, which reminds me that I need to buy more coffee at the store, and oh yes, while I'm out I should also stop at the pharmacy....whoa, focus: you're writing a book here!). We also have *financial, emotional,* and *perspective-taking* types of self-control (Lieberman, 2009).

Neuroscience has shown that the RVLPFC can be activated in a few different ways. But before we get into how it is activated, we need to first consider what stress looks like from a neuroscience perspective.

## The Neuroscience of Stress

The *stress cascade* is triggered when the amygdala, the emotional center of the brain, senses a threat (Carlson, 2013; Johnston & Olson, 2015). This activates the hippocampus, the seat of memory, which analyzes (in a split second) if we have seen this threat before, and a chain reaction involving the hypothalamus and the anterior cingulate cortex (ACC), which is uniquely connected to both the emotional centers of the limbic system and the frontal lobes (Goldberg, 2009). Once the ACC is engaged, it triggers the beginning of the *somatic* reactions to stress, by activating the sympathetic branch of the autonomic nervous system That's the point where it becomes noticeable that are having a reaction, particularly when you're scared, upset, or angry, and where you start to see physical changes in the body, such as an elevated heartbeat, trembling, or a lump in the pit of your stomach. These physiological events indicate that you are officially stressed, in the full mind and body sense.

It's at this stage, when the train has left the station and you're already in a state of stress, that the RVLPFC can do its magic—but only if we are able to activate it. And this is where knowledge is power, and why you're reading this chapter.

Neuroscience research shows that there are at least three interventions that activate the RVLPFC. These interventions are useful for communicators to know about for two different reasons: one, because they can be integrated as a form of *self-care*, so that communicators can better develop their own stress resilience, but second, as guidelines for designing more constructive communications, particularly when you need to communicate about difficult topics.

The three interventions are: *mindfulness, affect labeling*, and *cognitive reframing*. Together, I refer to them as the *neurocommunicator's toolkit*. Let's go through them one by one.

## Mindfulness

Mindfulness probably doesn't need much of an introduction, particularly as it seems to be riding a massive wave of popularity in the personal wellness space. There are now books, apps, and classes on everything from mindful eating to mindful sex. But mindfulness is not a fad—far from it. The neuroscience behind it is compelling and demonstrates unequivocal benefits for those who practice it regularly.

Most of the world's religious and spiritual traditions incorporate mindfulness and contemplative practices, including prayer and meditation. But there are many other, more secular forms of practice. These include mindful breathing, mindful walking, directed meditation, and mindful sense perception (such as focusing on visual and auditory experiences). There are also forms of mindful awareness and mindful appreciation (sometimes called *lovingkindness* meditation in the Buddhist tradition). The benefits of mindfulness practices are many and include improved learning and memory processes, emotional regulation, and perspective taking (Holzel et al., 2011).

One important thing to note is that mindfulness is not the same thing as relaxation. Mindfulness is about having a directed focus of attention, which requires effort and practice (there is an impressive but separate body of neuroscience research into relaxation and rest). Central to the practice of mindfulness is a sense of engagement of the mind with directed focus and intention.

The application of mindfulness to the workplace is relatively recent, but will hopefully become more widespread, particularly as organizations respond to increasing levels of fatigue, exhaustion, and stress. Studies have shown that anxiety and depression have become major diseases and employees also face high levels of *allostatic load*, from prolonged activation of the fight or flight response. Evidence suggests that mindfulness may protect the brain from these effects (Hassed, 2013).

Mindfulness, particularly when practiced regularly, has been shown to activate the RVLPFC (Lieberman, 2009; Tabibnia & Radecki, 2018). Mindfulness practitioners also experience many other significant and positive benefits in their brains, including less emotional reactivity, enhanced memory, and better access to their cognitive functions (Gotink et al., 2016; Kral et al., 2018).

While mindfulness sounds great, applying it to organizational communication presents some challenges. There are a few approaches communicators can take. One is by practicing mindfulness themselves, particularly as a self-care practice. Mindfulness is a remarkable tool for staying on your game and learning to roll with the punches that are an inevitable part of work and life. Mindfulness can also take the form of reflective practice. This also allows communicators to use their brains and their gut instincts better. Is this communication landing right? Does it convey the right tone? Does it promote a narrative that feels controversial or different? Just as firemen use their noses as much as their eyes, communicators need to consider how a communication feels rather than simply how it sounds or if it is grammatically correct.

On the organizational side, we can promote mindfulness by working with senior leaders to encourage them to promote more mindful behaviors. This includes things like encouraging breaks, trying to break the cycle of worry and rumination, engaging in appreciative inquiry, and helping employees become curious about ways we each show up at work, rather than merely reacting to it.

We can also focus on the body more, which is also a form of mindfulness. Incorporating more interoceptive and proprioceptive practices at team meetings.

Now that we've covered mindfulness, let's take a look at the intriguing art and science of naming our emotions.

## Affect Labeling (or Naming Emotions)

The next intervention that activates the RVLPFC is something referred to as *affect labeling*, which is the psychological term for "naming your emotions." Affect labeling has been shown to be a critical emotional regulation strategy (Lieberman, 2009; Tabibnia & Radecki, 2018; Torre & Lieberman, 2018).

Affect labeling is as simple as putting your feelings into words—but it is most effective when it describes not just the surface emotions but what might be lurking below (we often feel complex or even contradictory emotions at the same time). Affect labeling can also include noting the conscious and physical experience of having an emotion. Say, for example, you were to describe an emotion to an alien from outer space who didn't have a body and brain, how would you go about describing it? I'm feeling sad right now; what does sad actually feel like? What does it feel like in the body? Well, it feels heavy, it feels burdensome, I feel strain in my neck, I feel heaviness in my gut. Affect labeling allows you to take a deeper look at what an emotional experience is like and choose words to describe it.

A great technique for affect labeling, used a lot in psychotherapy and coaching, is to use the words "I observe" rather than "I am." So rather than saying, "I am sad," which is really labeling oneself as the emotion, instead we can say "I observe some sadness in myself today." I am observing some fear. I'm observing some trepidation as I go into this meeting with my boss. That's one way to practice affect labeling, and indeed mindfulness, at the same time.

Affect labeling is enormously powerful. It has been shown to reduce amygdala activity as well as activate the RVLPFC (Lieberman, 2009;

Lieberman et al., 2007). It may seem counterintuitive; there is a reluctance in many people to face and acknowledge their emotional experiences, particularly the painful ones, for fear of amplifying them. But neuroscience is validating what psychologists have known all along, which is that talking about and describing our emotional life goes a long way toward diffusing the power of its more maladaptive aspects. It enables us to become curious about ourselves and the way we interact with things and people, rather than being purely reactive.

Affect labeling can be used in organizational communications by acknowledging emotions when they are present but also by anticipating emotions that might show up. This type of communication is related to using the language of—you may have guessed—Affect (in the structural dynamics sense), which I discussed in Chapter 1. Affect allows us to be more authentic about the rich and varied emotional experiences of organizational life and helps to expand our behavioral repertoire around trust and authenticity.

When we are communicating about change, we can say things like, "It's natural to feel anxious when facing a change of this magnitude." A statement like that sounds small, but it can go a long way toward validating the experience of people facing the change, and signals to the organization that such emotions can be safely expressed. When people feel psychologically safe, they are much more likely to perform more effectively and be more engaged with their work (Edmondson, 2019).

Next, we'll take a look at the third intervention for engaging the RVLPFC. It is perhaps the most powerful tool in the neurocommunicator's toolkit: cognitive reframing.

## COGNITIVE REFRAMING

*Cognitive reframing* (sometimes called cognitive reappraisal or cognitive restructuring) is an emotional regulation technique that consists of identifying and then challenging irrational or maladaptive thoughts (Lieberman et al., 2011; Ochsner, 2013). It is a proven intervention for activation of the RVLPFC (Lieberman, 2009; Tabibnia & Radecki, 2018).

Maladaptive thoughts often take the form of cognitive distortions, which include faulty or inaccurate thinking or beliefs. Examples of cognitive distortions include overgeneralizations, black and white thinking, and jumping to conclusions—all of which are rampant in organizational life.

Cognitive distortions often have roots in childhood, and some distortions become ingrained habits that require patience and practice to overcome.

When we're able to do a cognitive reframe, we can identify and then challenge the cognition that's taking place. We can recognize the thought for what it is—a distortion—and develop more realistic and adaptive responses. Psychologists and coaches use cognitive reframing all the time, as do the best teachers and professors. Good bosses do too.

One of the most powerful reframes is recasting failure as a learning experience (Catalano et al., 2018; Lieberman et al., 2011). Organizations sometimes tacitly or explicitly signal a low tolerance for failure, even when the stakes aren't high, rather than being able to constructively reframe failure as a learning experience and explore the failure as an opportunity for discussion and growth. Leaders of organizations who consistently and courageously reframe failure not only facilitate higher degrees of collaboration and trust, they also enable higher levels of performance.

Another great way to reframe is to focus on what David Kantor referred to as the *structural story*, rather than the *moral story* (Kantor, 2012). The moral story is the story of blame, e.g., who did what to whom and how it led to a bad outcome. But the structural story (using the theory of structural dynamics) is one in which reflecting on the ways of showing up, the sets of hidden rules that were in use, and the "languages" people were speaking, enables us to recognize patterns and be better equipped to break out of them.

Another fantastic way to cognitively reframe is to consider the differences between *technical* and *adaptive* challenges. This is based on the principle of *adaptive leadership* and Ron Heifetz et al.'s (2009) seminal work at Harvard. Technical challenges are those that can be fixed easily, but adaptive challenges always require changes in people's priorities, beliefs, habits, and loyalties—and those changes are often painful. The problem with organizations is that most problems are mixed and have both adaptive and technical aspects. Using adaptive leadership can be a great way to reframe those problems and understand them through a better lens.

## THE NEUROCOMMUNICATOR'S TOOLKIT

Integrating the three interventions for RVLPFC activation—mindfulness, affect labeling, and cognitive reframing—is not necessarily an easy or natural approach for organizational communication. For example, posing reflective questions to employees in all-staff emails wouldn't work, nor would providing access to mindfulness apps as a pseudo-inoculation against exhaustion and burnout. But what does work is something that many communicators already use, even if they don't necessarily know the neuroscientific basis for it in neuroscience, and that is narration, or more specifically *storytelling*.

Storytelling in business communication has been studied for a long time, and is proven to be a highly effective technique, particularly for promoting trust in leadership, enhancing leader–follower dialogue, and creating psychological safety (Barker & Gower, 2010; Brown et al., 2005; Coyle, 2018). But storytelling isn't just for leaders; it is also effective for employees to share their stories with each other. I have used storytelling in various parts of this book to convey messages more effectively.

The author Dan Coyle (2018, p. 182), in his book *The Culture Code* wrote that "stories do not cloak reality but create it, triggering cascades of perception and motivation."

Infusing our stories with RVLPFC interventions has the potential to make them even more powerful, and through these stories we can start to see immediate benefits in terms of humanizing the experience of work and fostering deeper learning.

## References

Barker, R. T., & Gower, K. (2010). Strategic application of storytelling in organizations: Toward effective communication in a diverse world. *Journal of Business Communication, 47*(3), 295–312.

Brown, J. S., Denning, S., Groh, K., & Prusak, L. (2005). *Storytelling in organizations: Why storytelling is transforming 21st century organizations and management*. Elsevier Butterworth-Heinemann.

Carlson, N. R. (2013). *Physiology of behavior* (11th ed.). Pearson.

Catalano, A. S., Redford, K. H., Margolius, R., & Knight, A. T. (2018). Black swans, cognition and the power of learning from failure. *Conservation Biology, 32*(3), 584–596.

Coyle, D. (2018). *The culture code: The secrets of highly successful groups*. Bantam Books.

Edmondson, A. C. (2019). *The fearless organization: Creating psychological safety in the workplace for learning, innovation, and growth*. Wiley.

Goldberg, E. (2009). *The new executive brain: Frontal lobes in a complex world*. Oxford University Press.

Gotink, R. A., Meijboom, R., Vernooij, M. W., Smits, M., & Hunink, M. M. (2016). Eight-week mindfulness based stress reduction induces brain changes similar to traditional long- term meditation practice-a systematic review. *Brain and Cognition, 108,* 32–41.

Hassed, C. (2013). Mindfulness, well-being, and performance. In D. Rock & A. Ringleb (Eds.), *Handbook of neuroleadership* (pp. 225–240). Neuroleadership Institute.

Heifetz, R. A., Grashow, A., & Linsky, M. (2009). *The practice of adaptive leadership: Tools and tactics for changing your organization and the world.* Harvard Business Press.

Holzel, B. K., Lazar, S. W., Gard, T., Schuman-Olivier, Z., Vago, D. R., & Ott, U. (2011). How does mindfulness meditation work? Proposing mechanisms of action from a conceptual and neural perspective. *Perspectives on Psychological Science, 6,* 537–559.

Johnston, E., & Olson, L. (2015). *The feeling brain: The biology and psychology of emotions.* W.W. Norton & Company

Kantor, D. (2012). *Reading the room: Group dynamics for coaches and leaders.* Jossey-Bass.

Kral, T., Schuyler, B., Mumford, J., Rosenkranz, A., Lutz, A., & Davidson, R. (2018). Impact of short- and long-term mindfulness meditation training on amygdala reactivity to emotional stimuli. *NeuroImage, 181,* 301–313.

Lieberman, M. D. (2009). The brain's braking system (and how to 'use your words' to tap into it). *NeuroLeadership Journal, 2,* 9–14.

Lieberman M. D., Eisenberger N. I., Crockett M. J., Tom S. M., Pfeifer J. H., & Way B. M. (2007, May). Putting feelings into words: affect labeling disrupts amygdala activity in response to affective stimuli. *Psychological Science,18*(5), 421–428.

Lieberman, M. D., Inagaki, T. K., Tabibnia, G., & Crockett, M. J. (2011). Subjective responses to emotional stimuli during labeling, reappraisal, and distraction. *Emotion, 11*(3), 468–480.

Ochsner, K. (2013). Staying cool under pressure: Insights from social-cognitive neuroscience and their implications for self and society. In D. Rock & A. Ringleb (Eds.), *Handbook of neuroleadership* (pp. 193–204). Neuroleadership Institute.

Tabibnia, G., & Radecki, D. (2018). Resilience training that can change the brain. *Consulting Psychology Journal: Practice and Research, 70*(1), 59–88.

Torre, J. B., & Lieberman, M. D. (2018). Putting feelings into words: Affect labeling as implicit emotion regulation. *Emotion Review, 10,* 116–124.

CHAPTER 8

# The Culture Club: The Neuroscience of Pronouns

**Abstract** This chapter provides a brief introduction to intercultural competence and cultural neuroscience. We explore the psychological construct of *self-construal*, and how self-construal can be primed in the brain by using "*I*" or "*we*" pronouns. We introduce the concept of *neurocultural leadership*, and how a more agile and strategic use of pronouns can make organizational communication more effective. We'll also look at an excerpt of a famous political speech by Barack Obama to understand the power of pronoun agility in engaging audiences.

**Keywords** Intercultural competence · Cultural neuroscience · Self-construal · Neurocultural leadership · Pronoun agility

© The Author(s), under exclusive license to Springer Nature Singapore Pte Ltd. 2022
L. McHale, *Neuroscience for Organizational Communication*, https://doi.org/10.1007/978-981-16-7037-4_8

## Intercultural Competence

The multicultural and often global nature of modern organizations requires communicators and leaders to develop increasing levels of intercultural competence. Intercultural competence refers to effective and appropriate behavior and communication in intercultural situations (Deardorff, 2011). These include the attitudes and knowledge that support an individual's effective performance in various cultural contexts.

Intercultural competence is emerging as an increasingly critical skill in communication and leadership. When designing and delivering messages for a global audience or across cultures, communicators must navigate highly complex terrain.

One sticky area is language and the translation of messages. In my career, I can recall many instances of translations gone awry, and often quite humorously. In one case, for an all-staff email in a European company I worked for, there was intense disagreement over whether the plural of the word "*bonus*" was "*bonuses*" or "*boni*" (Fortunately for the English speakers, "bonuses" won). There are also tales of corporate tagline and marketing slogan mistranslations, particularly from English to Chinese and other Asian languages, though many of these may be an urban myth.

But even when we get the translations right, things can go wrong in other ways. Messages are misconstrued, the offense is even taken. Tone may feel impersonal or sometimes overly familiar. Welcome to the world of communicating across cultures. Thankfully, neuroscience can help.

## Cultural Neuroscience

*Cultural neuroscience* is an emerging interdisciplinary field that connects the research domains of brain science and intercultural relations (Warnick & Landis, 2015). Most cultural neuroscience research focuses on how culture shapes the brain, and in turn how the brain fits and modifies culture (Han & Ma, 2015). As such, this type of research draws from many fields, including cross-cultural and social psychology. But the remarkable advances in brain imaging are the real stars of the show and are transforming how we understand culture and behavior.

Before the advent of neuroscience, cross-cultural studies were languishing. Hofstede's (1980) groundbreaking work on cultural dimensions, as well as business applications, such as House et al.'s (2004) impressive GLOBE study, which analyzed the cultural, societal, organizational, and leadership differences of 62 societies around the world, are major contributions but feel rather dated. Even today, many approaches to cross-cultural research read more like an inventory of cultural differences than the study of a dynamic process that is continuously negotiated and renegotiated. However, the application of neuroscience provides an innovative, brain-based approach, which is bringing fresh energy to the field (Warnick & Landis, 2015).

Cultural neuroscientists study specific regions of interest in the brain that are implicated in certain behaviors, and they often test for *self-construal dominance* to understand the cultural differences between brains. In the next session, we will explore what this means and why communicators need to know about it.

## SELF-CONSTRUAL

Cultural neuroscience is a very complex field, but for the purposes of organizational communication, we are going to focus on one of the most interesting areas and that is the psychological construct known as *self-construal*. Self-construal refers to the relationship between the self and others, and more specifically the degree to which people see themselves as separate from or connected to others (Markus & Kitayama, 1991). Self-construal is generally categorized as either *independent* or *interdependent* and is measured through validated assessments and scales (Singelis, 1994; Gudykunst & Lee, 2003).

With independent self-construal, individuals generally seek to maintain independence and express their individuality; but with interdependent self-construal, individuals generally focus on attending to others and fitting in (Markus & Kitayama, 1991). However, both types of self-construal are present in everyone, a concept that is referred to as the "dual self" (Singelis et al., 1999). One type of self-construal might have salience in a certain context but not another (for example, an Asian-American visiting family in China), and its influence may be prolonged or more fleeting (Hong et al., 2003; Oyserman & Lee, 2008). Similarly, many individuals hold more flexible representations of the self and are quite agile in moving from one type of self-construal to the other (Hong et al., 2000; Ng et al., 2010). These individuals are often bilingual and have significant cross-cultural experience (Glazer et al., 2016).

Perhaps the easiest way to understand independent and interdependent self-construal is to compare them to their culture-level equivalents: *individualism* and *collectivism*.

Studies have found that Westerners (e.g., Americans, most Europeans) tend to have more independent self-construal, while Asians (e.g., Chinese, Koreans, and Japanese) tend to score higher in interdependent self-construal (Ng et al., 2010; Oyserman & Lee, 2008). In other words, people from Western cultures tend to be more individualistic, while those from Eastern cultures tend to be more collectivistic.

Self-construal is an important variable to study because influences a vast array of human experiences. For example, research has found that self-construal influences the basis for self-esteem (Singelis et al., 1999); emotional reactions toward injustice and punishment (Gollwitzer & Bücklein, 2007); and even if an apology likely to inspire forgiveness (Fehr & Gelfand, 2010). In one of the more intriguing studies, self-construal type predicted ethical behavior in leaders, as well as how followers perceive it (Hoyt & Price, 2015). Self-construal also influences very private aspects of an individual's experience of themselves in the world (Zhang et al., 2017). For people from cultures with independent self-construal, agency is attributed to the self, whereas in more interdependent cultures, agency is attributed to the group (Hess et al., 2016; Ito et al., 2013). And in organizational life, self-construal type has been shown to predict leadership communication style (Hackman et al., 1999).

Clearly, self-construal is an important construct to know about. But perhaps the most fascinating thing about it is that it is very easy to manipulate.

## How to Prime Self-Construal

Self-construal priming is a research technique that shifts the proportion of independent versus interdependent self-construal in individuals (Gardner et al., 1999). Even before modern neuroscience studies, different types of self-construal were thought to reside in different parts of the brain (Trafimow et al., 1997). A surprisingly high percentage of experiments in cultural neuroscience involve priming self-construal for the purposes of understanding how a shift from one style to the other produces changes in the brain. In most of the research I've read, there are two types of priming techniques: cultural symbols and pronoun manipulation.

Symbol priming involves using well-recognized and emotionally resonant images to produce a shift in self-construal, such as an American flag to prime for independent, or a Chinese-style dragon to prime for interdependent (Glazer et al., 2016). However, pronoun manipulation, which is much more common, involves much subtler means, such as Brewer and Gardner's (1996) pronoun word search task. This task involves reading a descriptive story that uses either singular (e.g., "I" and "you" for independent priming) or plural ("we" and "they" for interdependent priming) pronouns and highlighting them. This technique has been shown to be highly effective in shifting the balance between independent and interdependent self-construals (Gardner et al., 1999), and as a result, has been widely used in cultural neuroscience research.

Pronoun priming has been shown to produce changes beyond just self-construal. For example, one study found that people who vary their pronoun use in expressive writing reported significant improvements in physical and mental health (Seih et al., 2011). Clearly, there are many unsung benefits to being more agile in terms of pronoun use.

## WHY CULTURAL NEUROSCIENCE MATTERS FOR COMMUNICATORS

Why is this important for communicators? Well, first of all, we need to understand that pronouns impact people from different cultures in different ways. One-size-fits-all communications are not always going to be appropriate, and extra attention should be paid to pronouns, especially for more delicate messages that are delivered across a significant cultural divide. A smart way to anticipate some of the cultural differences, particularly if you aren't sure about a particular country, is to use online tools such as the Hofstede Insights country comparison or a similar resource.

Secondly, pronouns are powerful, and communicators should learn to use them to maximum effect. Pronoun agility is a skill we need to cultivate more, because it expresses a deeper resourcefulness and ability to shift perspective. In that sense, pronoun agility is not just a tool but a *practice* for developing what I refer to as *neurocultural leadership* (McHale, 2019).

Thirdly, we need to be more sophisticated about pronoun use. Many communicators are taught or encouraged to use "we" pronouns to promote group identity and belonging. Such advice is also common in the leadership literature, particularly for leaders who wish to develop a more transformational style (e.g., Molenberghs et al., 2017). One study from Germany showed a positive relationship between CEOs use of "we" language and key indicators of financial performance (Fladerer et al., 2021). The thinking is that using more "we" pronouns will enhance teamwork, a sense of shared ownership, and relationship-building, particularly because many workers experience challenges in collaborating with others and try to tough it out alone. This is a valid suggestion. *In Western contexts.*

The problem with this approach is that it can be counter-productive in other cultural contexts. It reveals a bias because it assumes that the audiences for communications are individualistic. That is not always the case, especially when we are communicating globally. For example, a fascinating study from mainland China found that priming "I" rather than "we" pronouns in Chinese research subjects increased levels of empathy for out-group (non-Chinese) members (Wang et al., 2015). In other words, "we" pronouns made the research subjects more biased, not less. Higher bias suggests that collaboration with out-group members would be substantially lower.

Neuroscience studies such as this provide clever tips for communicators, but they also provide empirical evidence for our communications strategies. Because of the research, we can surmise that "I" pronouns would probably be more effective than "we" pronouns in promoting collaboration across diverse groups in people from collectivistic cultures. For more individualistic cultures, we are probably better off trying to use more "we." Or better yet, being flexible with them both.

### *Obama's Speech on Race*

Now that we have developed a deeper appreciation of the neuroscience of pronouns, let's look at a masterful example of pronoun use in action.

Barack Obama's 2008 speech on race, delivered from the Philadelphia Constitution Center, was a pivotal moment in American political history. In the speech, Obama confronted the country's deep racial wounds within the context of American history more broadly, but also those of his own family and life experience.

It is also an illuminating example of pronoun agility, shifting from "we" and "us" to "I." Here is an excerpt:

This was one of the tasks we set forth at the beginning of this presidential campaign — to continue the long march of those who came before us, a march for a more just, more equal, more free, more caring and more prosperous America. I chose to run for president at this moment in history because I believe deeply that we cannot solve the challenges of our time unless we solve them together, unless we perfect our union by understanding that we may have different stories, but we hold common hopes; that we may not look the same and we may not have come from the same place, but we all want to move in the same direction — toward a better future for our children and our grandchildren.

This belief comes from my unyielding faith in the decency and generosity of the American people. But it also comes from my own story. (Obama, 2008)

In the next chapter, we will continue this exploration into pronouns, as well as other interesting words, and what they reveal about our organizations and culture.

## References

Brewer, M. B., & Gardner, W. (1996). Who is this "we"? Levels of collective identity and self representations. *Journal of Personality and Social Psychology, 71*(1), 83–93.

Deardorff, D. (2011). Assessing intercultural competence. *New Directions for Institutional Research, 149*, 65–79.

Fehr, R., & Gelfand, M. J. (2010). When apologies work: How matching apology components to victims' self-construals facilitates forgiveness. *Organizational Behavior and Human Decision Processes, 113*, 37–50.

Fladerer, M. P., Haslam, S. A., Steffens, N. K., & Frey, D. (2021). The value of speaking for "us": The relationship between CEOs' use of I- and we-referencing language and subsequent organizational performance. *Journal of Business and Psychology, 36*(2), 299–313.

Gardner, W. L., Gabriel, S., & Lee, A. Y. (1999). "I" value freedom, but "we" value relationships: Self-construal priming mirrors cultural differences in judgment. *Psychological Science, 10*, 321–326.

Glazer, S., Blok, S., Mrazek, A. J., & Mathis, A. M. (2016). Implications of behavioral and neuroscience research for cross-cultural training. In J. E. Warnick & D. N. Landis (Eds.), *Neuroscience in intercultural contexts* (pp. 171–202). Springer.

Gollwitzer, M., & Bücklein, K. (2007). Are "we" more punitive than "me"? Self-construal styles, justice-related attitudes, and punitive judgments. *Social Justice Research, 20,* 457–478.

Gudykunst, W. B., & Lee, C. M. (2003). Assessing the validity of self construal scales: A response to Levine et al. *Human Communication Research, 29*(2), 253–274.

Hackman, M. Z., Ellis, K., Johnson, C. E., & Staley, C. (1999). Self-construal orientation: Validation of an instrument and a study of the relationship to leadership communication style. *Communication Quarterly, 47,* 183–195.

Han, S., & Ma, Y. (2015). A culture-behavior-brain loop model of human development. *Trends in Cognitive Sciences, 9*(11), 666–676.

Hess, U., Blaison, C., & Kafetsios, K. (2016). Judging facial emotion expressions in context: The influence of culture and self-construal orientation. *Journal of Nonverbal Behavior, 40,* 55–64.

Hofstede, G. (1980). *Culture's consequences: International differences in work-related values.* Sage.

Hong, Y., Benet-Martinez, V., Chiu, C., & Morris, M. (2003). Boundaries of cultural influence: Construct activation as a mechanism for cultural differences in social perception. *Journal of Cross-Cultural Psychology, 34*(4), 453–464.

Hong, Y., Morris, M. W., Chiu, C., & Benet-Martinez, V. (2000). Multicultural minds: A dynamic constructivist approach to culture and cognition. *American Psychologist, 55,* 709–720.

House, R. J., Hanges, P. J., Javidan, M., Dorfman, P. W., & Gupta, V. (Eds.). (2004). *Culture, leadership, and organizations: The GLOBE study of 62 societies.* Sage.

Hoyt, C. L., & Price, T. L. (2015). Ethical decision making and leadership: Merging social role and self-construal perspectives. *Journal of Business Ethics, 127*(4), 531–539.

Ito, K., Masuda, T., & Li, L. M. W. (2013). Agency and facial emotion judgment in context. *Personality and Social Psychology Bulletin, 39*(6), 763–776.

Markus, H. R., & Kitayama, S. (1991). Culture and the self: Implications for cognition, emotion and motivation. *Psychological Review, 98,* 224–253.

McHale, L. E. (2019). *The neurocultural leader: Developing self-construal agility for intercultural competency.* Doctoral dissertation. ProQuest Dissertations Publishing (UMI No. 13863797).

Molenberghs, P., Prochilo, G., Steffens, N. K., Zacher, H., & Haslam, S. A. (2017). The neuroscience of inspirational leadership: The importance of collective-oriented language and shared group membership. *Journal of Management, 43*(7), 2168–2194.

Ng, S. H., Han, S., Mao, L., & Lai, J. C. (2010). Dynamic bicultural brains: FMRI study of their flexible neural representation of self and significant others in response to culture primes. *Asian Journal of Social Psychology, 13,* 83–91.

Obama, B. (2008, March 18). *A more perfect union* [Speech transcript]. Philadelphia Constitution Center. https://www.npr.org/templates/story/story.php?storyId=88478467

Oyserman, D., & Lee, S. W. S. (2008). Does culture influence what and how we think? Effects of priming individualism and collectivism. *Psychological Bulletin, 134*(2), 311–342.

Seih, Y.-T., Chung, C. K., & Pennebaker, J. W. (2011). Experimental manipulations of perspective taking and perspective switching in expressive writing. *Cognition & Emotion, 25,* 926–938.

Singelis, T. M. (1994). The measurement of independent and interdependent self-construals. *Personality and Social Psychology Bulletin, 20*(5), 580–591.

Singelis, T. M., Bond, M. H., Sharkey, W. F., & Lai, C. (1999). Unpacking culture's influence on self-esteem and embarrassability. *Journal of Cross-Cultural Psychology, 30,* 315–341.

Trafimow, D., Silverman, E. S., Fan, R. M. T., & Law, J. S. F. (1997). The effects of language and priming on the relative accessibility of the private self and the collective self. *Journal of Cross-Cultural Psychology, 28,* 107–123.

Wang, C., Wu, B., Liu, Y., Wu, X., & Han, S. (2015). Challenging emotional prejudice by changing self-concept: Priming independent self-construal reduces racial in-group bias in neural responses to other's pain. *Social Cognitive and Affective Neuroscience, 10*(4), 1115–1201.

Warnick, J. E., & Landis, D. (2015). *Neuroscience in intercultural contexts.* Springer.

Zhang, T., Xi, S., Jin, Y., & Wu, Y. (2017). Self-construal priming modulates self-evaluation under social threat. *Frontiers in Psychology, 8,* 1759.

CHAPTER 9

# More on the Neuroscience of Words

**Abstract** This chapters continues the exploration of pronouns by examining pronoun use in the political speech. We explore the differences between the inclusive and exclusive "we," and the perils of the overuse of "I." We discuss modal words, both strong and weak (the latter sometimes called weasel words). We review the emerging field of data mining and sentiment analysis. Lastly, we discuss the need for a more authentic language of vulnerability in organizational life.

**Keywords** Modal words · Data mining · Sentiment analysis · Clusivity

## The Politics of Pronouns

As we saw in the last chapter and in the excerpt of Obama's speech on race, analyzing political speech is a worthwhile way to study pronouns, especially now that we understand how they work from a neuroscientific perspective. Pronoun use can be both subtle and profound so it's worth exploring the topic more deeply, especially since it's such a rich and relevant area for professional communication.

There is an impressive body of research into how politicians use pronouns, which is usually in a strategic way to show power, solidarity, or authority (Bull & Fetzer, 2006; Pennycook, 1994). For example, in Brozin's (2010) analysis of the Obama speech on race, he found that Obama displayed a preference for "we" pronouns to position himself as a spokesperson for the nation. He tended to use "I" pronouns in more mitigated phrases, such as "I believe" and "I cannot," which signaled, respectively, more or less personal involvement.

Pronouns in political speech are commonly used by politicians to construct favorable images of themselves and others (Bramley, 2001). Pronouns can be cleverly deployed to show affiliation or create distance between people. Bramley (2001) shrewdly observed that pronouns are used to *socially construct* the identity of the politician and others, rather than objectively represent them. This is a remarkably insightful point, because it emphasizes how political realities are co-created and collectively maintained through language choices.

### *The Nationalist "We"*

Pronoun use is also strongly influenced by culture and political orientation. For example, "we" pronouns are used extensively, sometimes exclusively, in mainland China and Communist Party rhetoric, usually to frame discourse within a nationalist context (Karlsson, 2017).

Let's take an example of a speech delivered by Xi Jinping to the World Economic Forum in January 2021. Here is an excerpt:

> The right approach is to act on the vision of a community with a shared future for mankind. We should uphold the common values of humanity, i.e. peace, development, equity, justice, democracy and freedom, rise above ideological prejudice, make the mechanisms, principles and policies of our cooperation as open and inclusive as possible, and jointly safeguard world

peace and stability. We should build an open world economy, uphold the multilateral trading regime, discard discriminatory and exclusionary standards, rules and systems, and take down barriers to trade, investment and technological exchanges. We should strengthen the G20 as the premier forum for global economic governance, engage in closer macroeconomic policy coordination, and keep the global industrial and supply chains stable and open. We should ensure the sound operation of the global financial system, promote structural reform and expand global aggregate demand in an effort to strive for higher quality and stronger resilience in global economic development. (Xi, 2021)

In this example, there are four instances of "we." I did a quick analysis of the full speech (it is approximately 3000 words—a little shorter than the average chapter in this book). In the full speech there were 47 instances of "we," four instances of "they" and four instances of "us." There was nary an "I" pronoun in the entire speech. According to Karlsson (2017), this is not unusual for Chinese political speeches.

Just to see what would happen, in a very non-scientific experiment, I swapped out the "we" pronouns for "I." and have indicated the changes in bold text below:

The right approach is to act on the vision of a community with a shared future for mankind. **I** should uphold the common values of humanity, i.e. peace, development, equity, justice, democracy and freedom, rise above ideological prejudice, make the mechanisms, principles and policies of our cooperation as open and inclusive as possible, and jointly safeguard world peace and stability. **I** should build an open world economy, uphold the multilateral trading regime, discard discriminatory and exclusionary standards, rules and systems, and take down barriers to trade, investment and technological exchanges. **I** should strengthen the G20 as the premier forum for global economic governance, engage in closer macroeconomic policy coordination, and keep the global industrial and supply chains stable and open. **I** should ensure the sound operation of the global financial system, promote structural reform and expand global aggregate demand in an effort to strive for higher quality and stronger resilience in global economic development.

It is striking how much the use of "I" pronouns changes the emotional tenor of the speech. The pronoun "I"—can suggest a sort of manic grandiosity that was not present in the original speech, e.g., I don't think any sane politician would ever say "I should build an open world economy". But in other cases, the use of "I" conveys a sense of personal responsibility and accountability that is reassuring, e.g., "I should uphold the common values of humanity". This is instructive, because it reveals how pronoun use conveys—and sometimes reveals, other times obscures—a leader's sense of self in the systemic context.

In the research on political language, the reliance on "we" is even more illuminating for the ways it can manipulate and what it can obscure. Often, it implies *consensus* or a collective mandate where none may actually exist. The use of "we" can be a method by which leaders seek to gain legitimacy.

But "we" pronouns are even more complex than that because there are really two different kinds of "we" in speech, which we will review in the next section.

## Inclusive Versus Exclusive "We"

There are two different aspects of "we" pronouns: inclusive or exclusive. This concept is referred to as *clusivity*, which references whether the speaker is including the audience (the receiver of the communication) and others in the purview of the "we" (Filimonova, 2005).

An example of the exclusive "we" might be, "We the Communications team." It is used to *distinguish* one group from another. But the inclusive "we" is meant to reference pretty much everyone (whether this is actually true or not). A famous example from my own country is, "We the people."

It gets a little confusing because the "we" can be inclusive in some respects and then exclusive in others. For example, being Scottish in Scotland is an inclusive, "We are Scottish," but in a political discussion, it might become an exclusive "we" to distinguish it from other parts of the UK.

The inclusive "we," is quite expansive and usually signals broad commonalities of experience. How it is used can really vary, depending on the optics; it can appear rather brazen to speak on behalf of everyone, at least in non-totalitarian contexts. More typically, instead of the inclusive "we," communicators will reference universal ideas and principles, such as "mental health" or "justice" or "humanity." The inclusive "we" is increasingly seen in the language around climate change, e.g., "We must do something to address climate change", meaning *everyone* must. This sense of inclusiveness is also implied as a core principle in many forms of jurisprudence, including such legal concepts as *crimes against humanity* and *hostis humani generis* (for more on these, please see Green, 2008).

In political speech, the inclusive or exclusive "we" is usually made explicit through the context. But not always. Sometimes it's left a little vague on purpose. Who is the "we" we are talking about? It's also interesting when politicians abandon the exclusive "we" and shift to the third person; "folks" is a common one in American political rhetoric, or even more euphemistic choices, such as "Second Amendment people." This is a particularly crafty way of acknowledging, and sometimes tacitly nodding to, specific groups without explicitly signaling membership within them. More adaptively, it can be used to signal that there is dissent or a different opinion.

The wishy-washy "we" (have I coined an alliteration?) also happens in organizations, with surprising frequency. Leaders sometimes obliquely reinforce the status and privileges of certain groups within organizations, while neglecting others (usually without realizing they are doing it). This commonly happens in a racial/cultural or gender sense, especially because organizations tend to mirror the larger inequalities that exist in the societies in which they are embedded. But it also involves internal politics and the often unacknowledged status and privilege connected to job type and department. Organizations have high status and low-status roles, and many in between. Sometimes, leaders (and employees) talk about core businesses using an exclusive "we", but infrastructure functions such as Compliance, HR, Risk, and Communications become "they" or "them"—unless the leader switches back to a more inclusive "we." This type of pronoun use conveys subtle but potent messages about belonging and what teams have a legitimate stake in an organization's success.

Why is this important for communicators? For a few reasons. We know from the SCARF™ and SCOAP models that Status and Relatedness are stress/reward triggers and Attachment is a core human need. The exclusive "we" may reward Status for the ingroup members, but it threatens Status for the outgroup—especially those that want to belong. For outgroup members, the exclusive "we" meddles with the sense of Relatedness and creates insecure Attachment. Those not included in the "we" (an experience common for generations of non-White Americans, for example), have a sense of not belonging or feeling welcome. This activates all the pain centers of the brain. It is a pernicious influence in our organizations and can frustrate everything from our strategies to create more creative and collaborative cultures to diversity and inclusion initiatives.

That said, the exclusive "we" is always going to be prevalent in organizational communications. After all, these are messages on behalf of a group of people working in concert, engaged in a collective endeavor. External communications and Marketing professionals rely on it: "We are committed to delivering the best solutions" or "We take your feedback seriously."

But for more internally focused communications, we need to be particularly mindful of how the use of "we" can impact messaging, particularly for leadership communication. As we have seen, pronouns can be used to strengthen or disrupt the relationships between CEOs and employees (Warnick, 2010). They can also serve to disenfranchise people, functions, and roles.

## The Perils of "I"

Now let's turn to the use of "I" pronouns, which are equally fascinating. Just as overuse of "we" can pose certain risks for organizations, the overuse of "I" is particularly revealing for leadership communications.

Both within organizations and in the world at large, the words of politicians, central bankers, and CEOs are carefully, even painstakingly, parsed for clues around the person's intent, personality, and leadership style.

There is a growing body of evidence that the heavy use of "I" pronouns in leadership communications is linked to narcissism and other maladaptive leadership syndromes. For example, one study explored the link between CEO language and hubristic leadership, particularly as associated with unethical and destructive behaviors (Akstinaite et al., 2019). Another study explored the ratio of "I" to "we" pronouns in CEO communication as an effective proxy for CEO narcissism (Aabo et al., 2020). And a third study focused on the size of CEO signatures and their relationship to narcissism and poor financial performance (Ham et al., 2018).

The heavy use of "I" pronouns can signal that something is seriously amiss with an organization's leadership. Often it signals a more heroic mode of leadership, rather than viewing leadership as a distributed function (Heifetz et al., 2009). With an over-reliance on "I" pronouns, there can be a pervasive sense of unease, uncertainty, and fear throughout the organization. These are powerful stress triggers for the brain. Obviously, in these types of toxic environments, the communications themselves may be the least unsettling aspects of working there, even as we see how communication can serve as a barometer of the relative health of leadership and the long-term stability of an organization.

## Strong Modals and Weasel Words

It's not just pronoun use that is fascinating in this way. There is also some terrific research on the use of *modal words* in organizational communications. I was surprised to see that most of this research is published in accounting and finance journals and not those related to communication, leadership, or organizational psychology. Which is all the more reason that it's worthwhile for communicators to take a multidisciplinary approach.

A *modal* is a grammatical term used to describe a word that is used with a verb to express possibility or intention. Modal words are usually described as *strong* or *weak*, depending on the degree of certainty that they signal. For example, weak modal words are terms such as *may, might, could, depending, possibly*, and *appears*, and signal less certainty than strong modal words such as *can, will, shall*, and *are*. Weak modal words are also known, more colloquially, as *weasel words* (Loughran & McDonald, 2016).

Studies have shown that the use of modal words in corporate communications can be an important measure of a company's financial health. For example, one study of publicly traded American firms showed that companies with a high proportion of weak modal words in their annual reports and/or IPO prospectuses showed higher subsequent stock return volatility than firms that did not (Loughran & McDonald, 2016). This insight makes a compelling case for textual analysis as part of an investment strategy.

Organizations understandably tend to downplay negative news in their formal communications, and often carefully couch it among other, more positive messages. The problem with this approach is that negative information is so padded with positive words that the overall meaning becomes obscure. This is a big problem for investors and financial analysts alike. To solve this conundrum, two Finance professors at the University of Notre Dame, Tim Loughran and Bill McDonald, conducted a sweeping textual analysis of American corporate 10-Ks (e.g., annual reports) over a ten-year period, to see if they could ferret out ways that companies employed avoidance strategies in their communications. They evaluated *expressions of sentiment* and created six different (and often overlapping) word lists to categorize them: Negative, Positive, Uncertainty, Litigious, Strong modal, and Weak modal. Their overall goal was to identify words that signal avoidance strategies in communication style (Loughran & McDonald, 2011).

The resulting Loughran and McDonald (LM) sentiment lexicon is extensive. The biggest lists are of the Positive and Negative words; they found over 300 Positive and 2300 Negative words. Given that ratio, it is plain to see how many organizations will take great pains to invent countless ways of describing negative events, often at the expense of simple and straightforward language.

By the way, the ten most frequently occurring LM Negative words are: *loss, losses, claims, impairment, against, adverse, restated, adversely, restructuring*, and *litigation*. These ten words represent less than 1% of the LM universe of words, yet they account for more than 33% of the negative words which appeared in American 10-Ks (Loughran & McDonald, 2011).

Based on their analysis, Loughran and McDonald (2011) argued that the *readability of financial documents* could be a reliable predictor of return volatility, as well as a predictor of forecast errors and earnings forecast dispersion among financial analysts. But the biggest takeaway from the LM dictionary is that language matters, *especially in times of stress or turmoil*, and that many organizations have a problem with communicating in a way that is transparent, straightforward, and open.

The LM dictionary is most pertinent to investor relations and the communication of financial results. But these types of words creep into all types of organizational communication, and not just publicly traded companies. There are important lessons here for internal communications as well, which we will explore more closely in the next section.

## Text Mining and Sentiment Analysis

The LM dictionary project is part of an emerging field known as *text mining*, sometimes referred to as *natural language processing*. Text mining is a research technique that uses computer algorithms to extract useful information and patterns from large amounts of textual data (Das et al., 2019). *Sentiment analysis*, like that done by Loughran and McDonald, is a sub-field of text mining, which focuses on the sentiments or opinions contained in a piece of text (Liu, 2020). Some researchers are using text mining and sentiment analysis to study the communications patterns of organizations to see if, among other things, they can create a possible early warning system of fraudulent business activity (Das et al., 2019).

The Enron debacle provides a riveting example of what this research can yield. In the aftermath of Enron's implosion, the US Federal Energy Regulatory Commission released a treasure trove of information, including Enron's corporate communications and internal emails for a two-year period leading up to the firm's collapse. In an analysis of over 100,000 emails sent by Enron employees, as well as over 1000 articles that appeared on *PR Newswire* from January 2000 to December 2001, Das et al. (2019) found that these corporate communications effectively predicted the crisis. They did this by measuring how positive sentiment declined both internally and externally. But even more interestingly, they found that certain structural characteristics, such as average email length and number of emails sent, were even stronger predictors of trouble than the sentiment analysis. A striking finding was, for one 13-week period, that for every 20-character decline in email length, there was a 1.2% drop in stock price—in fact, email length declined by 50% into 2001. However, even though emails were shorter, senior executives at Enron communicated more frequently, a trend presaging the coming collapse (Das et al., 2019).

The beauty of textual analysis is that it avoids the privacy concerns around reading individual employee emails because its treats datasets systematically and searches for broader trends. As such, Das et al. (2019) believe that regular sentiment and structural email analysis would be an important risk management strategy for organizations and regulators 2019.

## The Importance of Clarity

My purpose with this chapter is not to condemn certain words or to urge communicators to police their language more rigidly. Rather, I want to encourage communicators become more curious about the words that they use and what they say about our organizations. When weak modal words come up in our communication, for example, we need to get curious about why we are using them, what kind of information we might be seeking to avoid acknowledging, and whether we—and our organizations—would be better served by choosing words that are more straightforward and candid.

After all, we can see how sentiment analysis provides important clues as to what is going on in an organization and text mining proves that organizational communication is a uniquely effective barometer of an organization's health.

But Curiosity also allows us to laugh. Some of the euphemisms, verbal gymnastics, and linguistic contortions that politicians and companies come up with are really very funny, even as they can be infuriating—particularly when they signal deep divisions and outright dishonesty. This is one of the reasons that former *Financial Times* columnist Lucy Kellaway's scathing takedowns of corporate language, or what she referred to as *claptrap* or *guff*, were so satisfying.

From a neuroscience and psychology perspective, what can we learn from this? What might be going on in the brain and body when we hear weak or strong modal words, or receive emails that are curt and inscrutable? For me, the first thing that comes to mind is *ethos*, in the Aristotelian framework. The integrity of the communicator is called into question. This ties to the structural dynamics language of Power, which, when ascendant is about competence, optimism and skill, but its shadow can be "win-at-all-costs" and corrupt (Kantor, 2012).

It also says something about how we deal, as individuals and organizations, with vulnerability. There is a type of vulnerability, described so well in Brené Brown's (2019) work, which is emotionally authentic, facilitates connection, and enables compassion. But there is a less courageous type of vulnerability, that uses evasion and even deceit to conceal itself. This type of vulnerability, even when it's subtle, triggers a powerful threat response in the brain, causing that sense of something not being quite right. From a SCARF™ perspective, it threatens our need for Certainty, but it can also tread on our needs for Autonomy and Fairness.

Organizations, like people, often have defense mechanisms that protect them from facing uncomfortable or difficult emotions (Obholzer & Roberts, 2019). But just like for people, true well-being comes from facing our demons, acknowledging our fears, and summoning the courage to meet the challenges we encounter. This is the place where transformative growth comes from and is the topic of our next chapter.

## References

Aabo, T., Als, M., Thomsen, L., & Wulff, J. N. (2020). Watch me go big: CEO narcissism and corporate acquisitions. *Review of Behavioral Finance*, 43 pages.

Akstinaite, V., Robinson, G., & Sadler-Smith, E. (2019). Linguistic markers of CEO hubris. *Journal of Business Ethics*, 167(4), 687–705.

Bramley, N. R. (2001). *Pronouns of politics: The use of pronouns in the construction of 'self' and 'other' in political interviews*. Ph.D. thesis. Australia National University.

Brown, B. (2019). *Dare to lead: Brave work, tough conversations, whole hearts*. Random House.

Brozin, M. (2010, September). *The intentions behind Barack Obama's strategic use of personal pronouns*. C-thesis English linguistics. http://www.diva-portal.org/smash/get/diva2:375134/FULLTEXT01.pdf

Bull, P., & Fetzer, A. (2006). Who are we and who are you? The strategic use of forms of address in political interviews. *Text Talk*, 26(1), 3–37.

Das, S. R., Kim, S., & Kothari, B. (2019). Zero-revelation RegTech: Detecting risk through linguistic analysis of corporate emails and news. *The Journal of Financial Data Science*, 1(2), 8–34.

Filimonova, E. (Ed.). (2005). *Clusivity: Typology and case studies of inclusive-exclusive distinction*. John Benjamin.

Greene, J. (2008). Hostis humani generis. *Critical Inquiry*, 34(4), 683–705.

Ham, C., Seybert, N., & Wang, S. (2018). Narcissism is a bad sign: CEO signature size, investment, and performance. *Review of Accounting Studies*, 23, 234–264.

Heifetz, R. A., Grashow, A., & Linsky, M. (2009). *The practice of adaptive leadership: Tools and tactics for changing your organization and the world*. Harvard Business Press.

Kantor, D. (2012). *Reading the room: Group dynamics for coaches and leaders*. Jossey-Bass.

Karlsson, S. (2017). *Passing on the torch: Discourse strategies in the inaugural speeches of Jiang, Hu and Xi*. Master's thesis, Uppsala University.

Liu, S. (2020) *Document-level sentiment analysis of email data*. Ph.D. thesis, James Cook University.

Loughran, T., & McDonald, B. (2011). When is a liability not a liability? Textual analysis, dictionaries, and 10-Ks. *Journal of Finance*, 66(1), 35–65.

Loughran, T., & McDonald, B. (2016). Textual analysis in accounting and finance: A survey. *Journal of Accounting Research*, 54, 1187–1230.

Obholzer, A., & Roberts, V. Z. (2019). *The unconscious at work: A Tavistock approach to making sense of organizational life*. Routledge.

Pennycook, A. (1994, April). The politics of pronouns. *ELT Journal*, 48(2), 173–178.

Xi, J. (2021, January 25). *Special address by Chinese President Xi Jinping at the World Economic Forum* [Speech transcript]. Via video link from Beijing, China. Retrieved August 26, 2021, from http://www.xinhuanet.com/english/2021-01/25/c_139696610.htm

Warnick, Q. (2010). A close textual analysis of corporate layoff memos. *Business Communication Quarterly, 73*, 322–326.

CHAPTER 10

# The Neuroscience of Compassion

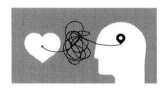

**Abstract** This chapter explores the concept of *vicarious traumatization* and how it can be an occupational hazard for professional communicators. We explore post-traumatic organizational growth, and the psychology of grieving and loss. Lastly, we discuss how communicators can use awareness of these concepts to serve as change agents and help unlock energy in their organizations.

**Keywords** Vicarious traumatization · Post-traumatic organizational growth · Grieving · Loss

\* \* \*

Neuroscience has shown, if we did not know already, that we have rich emotional lives. Exquisitely sensitive to our environments—both physical and social—it is impossible for us to separate the experience of feeling from what it is to be alive (Lewis et al., 2001).

In the last chapter, I talked about how we deal with vulnerability, whether we deny it, acknowledge it, or somewhere in between. But vulnerability speaks to a larger issue of how we equip ourselves for the challenges we face in the communications profession. Especially how we are equipped psychologically. An important aspect of this is trauma.

## VICARIOUS TRAUMATIZATION

Communicators are often tasked with communicating around bad news. This can include more common occurrences, such as oversight failures, accidents, and job redundancies, but it also can include rarer events involving tragedy and death. Every so often, communicators must cope with a full-blown crisis. Such experiences can be watershed events in a communicator's career. There is no other time that organizational communication is more important or impactful.

As most professional communicators are aware, preparation is essential. Having a well thought out crisis comms strategy before you need it is worth the time and energy it requires to create one. But often we aren't equipped to prepare ourselves emotionally for these types of events. We cannot anticipate how we might be personally impacted, or how that might influence our ability to communicate in an emotionally coherent way that is of service to employees, leaders, and an organization's key stakeholders.

With certain types of crisis communications, communicators are at higher risk of developing what psychologists refer to as *vicarious traumatization*. Generally, trauma is understood to be both primary and secondary. Primary trauma involves direct exposure, such as what happens in the military or with first responders, such as firemen and the police. Secondary trauma is trauma that is experienced more vicariously, through hearing about, reading about, seeing news coverage of, or discussing traumatic events with others. This latter type of trauma is a well-recognized syndrome, often experienced by psychologists and doctors who care for traumatized others (Maitlis, 2020). It is also very common, and receiving increased and deserved attention, among journalists (Specht & Tsilman, 2018).

However, the role of vicarious trauma in communicators has been under-explored. It is a topic typically not included in training programs, academic curricula, or industry conferences.

This needs to change. Communicators cope with their own emotional reactions to trauma but they also have an enormous responsibility in terms of designing and delivering organizational messages pertaining to it. This dual experience is often both a burden and an honor.

One of my own experiences of trauma came from my work for an organization with offices at the World Trade Center on September 11, 2001. My organization lost several employees and our offices were destroyed. Because I was not actually in the office that morning, my trauma was vicarious and not primary. But I experienced significant vicarious trauma by drafting communications about the tragedy, gathering information, interviewing survivors, and crafting messages. The first all-staff email of my career was drafted two weeks after 9/11. I still remember my hands shaking as I typed it.

In the months and years that followed, I was often tasked with drafting organizational and leadership communications pertaining to the terror attacks and their aftermath, especially annual commemorations of the employees whose lives were lost. I approached such work with dread but also humility. It was important work, of which I am proud, but it was always grueling to produce.

Events don't have to be on the scale of September 11 or other terror attacks to inspire vicarious traumatization. Smaller-scale losses, such as the death of a colleague or leader, can be likewise profound. But in all cases, it's important to remember that these are losses on both the individual and organizational levels.

It is well understood that in the aftermath of a trauma, survivors are often haunted by feelings of anxiety, anger, sadness, and guilt. Severe trauma can interfere with a person's ability to self-regulate, resulting in diminished cognitive capacity and focus (Van der Kolk, 2014). Survivors frequently have aftershocks of these emotions, which at times can be overwhelming and difficult to control. They are also sensitive to reminders of the traumatic event, making commemorative communications particularly tricky.

Research on organizational trauma makes it clear that one of the things that makes a traumatic event so devastating is the sense of a loss of safety in the world (Maitlis, 2020). However, over time, usually, the individual learns how to regulate their emotional reactions and recover that safety. It is in this recovery that organizational communication can play a powerful role.

## *Post-Traumatic Organizational Growth*

Occupational support plays an important role in recovery from trauma (Brooks et al., 2019; Frost, 2003; Maitlis, 2020). Organizations with healthy cultures are able to foster recovery more quickly. In such workplaces, employees are treated with care and compassion, and, in turn, they tend to reciprocate with higher levels of commitment and job satisfaction (Maitlis, 2020).

Communicators who need to design messages around trauma can leverage research into validated approaches that help individuals make sense of trauma and begin the process of post-traumatic growth. These can be easily incorporated into organizational messages, and they will be familiar to readers of the previous chapters, especially after learning about the SCARF™ and SCOAP models and the neurocommunicator's toolkit. For our purposes here, we are looking at the same strategies but through more of a mental health and organizational wellness lens.

Sally Maitlis (2020), a professor at the Saïd Business School at Oxford, has identified several ways that organizations can help promote what she refers to as *post-traumatic organizational growth*. Each involves a form of *sensemaking*, a form of *cognitive reframing* which we discussed in Chapter 7:

- Sensemaking as cognition: making meaning from the event through thought, such as acceptance, downward comparison, or interpreting the event through one's own spiritual beliefs.
- Sensemaking as action: where individuals understand what has happened to them through the lens of the insights and lessons they have learned.
- Sensemaking as narrative: using narrative or stories about positive transformation, growth, or awakening.

All three aspects of sensemaking can be integrated into organizational and leadership communications and they each have the added benefit of being therapeutic for communicators themselves.

## Loss and Grieving

Even apart from major trauma, our emotional lives can pose many challenges in terms of how we show up. Organizations, like people, tend to tacitly encourage and reward particular behaviors and emotions, while discouraging others (Kantor, 2012). Those who do not stay within the bounds violate the rules of conduct, both written and unwritten.

But much of our emotional life at work is more subtle than that. Most of us invest a great deal of energy actively managing how we think we are being perceived by others, a concept psychologists refer to as *impression management*. It's another job you didn't know you had (Kegan & Lahey, 2009). But no matter how much we attempt to repress the emotional self, it still shows up, often in unpredictable ways. We may have unmet needs. Sometimes we are grieving. Always, we are coping with loss.

Heifetz et al. (2009), in their work on adaptive leadership, emphasized that people do not fear change so much as they fear loss—and loss is everywhere. Life involves loss. Work involves loss. We lose jobs, clients, teams, colleagues, and projects. We lose networks and support systems. Sometimes we lose money. We lose status. We even lose our identity, when we change roles, retire, or venture into a new career, even when those changes are desired and sought. Most of these losses are not adequately grieved, they go unacknowledged and under-explored.

The British psychotherapist Jody Day (2016) wisely observed that modern societies have become grief-phobic and grief-illiterate. Many aspects of grief, such as childlessness or the loss of a pet, are *disenfranchised*, meaning they are not commonly recognized as legitimate (Day, 2016). But we are grief-illiterate in more general ways as well; grieving tends to be viewed more as a private experience than a social process. This is a mistake, according to Day, because grief can only be healed in dialogue with others.

This is a critical concept to grasp for communication. In so much of our organizational lives, we promulgate messages of unrelenting positivity even when the messages themselves convey sad or disturbing news. This is not unique to organizations, but reflects a trend in the broader culture, one sometimes referred to as *toxic positivity* (Chiu, 2020). This positivity belies the sadness that can sometimes accompany us, in life and as we work. But it also belies the richness of our emotional experience more generally.

## Unlocking Energy

Many communicators seek to become change agents in their organizations. One of the best ways they can do so is by embracing a more expansive view of emotional experience at work. When we do things like acknowledging fear, acknowledge loss, and acknowledge grief, we not only signal to others that emotional authenticity is safe, but we change the brain itself. Some of this change is related to affect labeling, which we discussed in Chapter 6, a powerful intervention that activates the RVLPFC, helping to regulate the stress response. But it's also related to the cognitive and affective energy we save when we are no longer working so hard to repress our emotions (Kegan & Lahey, 2009). We unlock energy, in individuals as well as collectively. It makes us smarter, shrewder, and better able to meet the challenges we confront.

This practice also helps us develop compassion. Compassion for ourselves and how deeply we feel and sometimes suffer. Compassion for others.

What happens at work is really a combination of two things: the individual choices we make in terms of how we show up, and the nature of the culture in which we find ourselves embedded (Block, 2016). Choosing to show up more compassionately not only positions us as change agents, but helps us embody our leadership, showing that change, healing, and growth do not just happen in our prefrontal cortex: they are full brain and body events. And when we bring our full selves to work, anything is possible.

## References

Block, P. (2016). *The empowered manager: Positive political skills at work* (2nd ed.). Wiley.

Brooks, S. K., Rubin, G. J., & Greenberg, N. (2019). Traumatic stress within disaster-exposed occupations: Overview of the literature and suggestions for the management of traumatic stress in the workplace. *British Medical Bulletin, 129*, 25–34.

Chiu, A. (2020). Time to ditch 'toxic positivity,' experts say: 'It's okay not to be okay.' *The Washington Post*. https://www.washingtonpost.com/lifestyle/wellness/toxic-positivity-mental-health-covid/2020/08/19/5dff8d16-e0c8-11ea-8181-606e603bb1c4_story.html

Day, J. (2016). *Living the life unexpected: Twelve weeks to your Plan B for a meaningful and fulfilling future without children*. Bluebird.

Frost, P. J. (2003). *Toxic emotions at work: How compassionate managers handle pain and conflict*. Harvard Business School Press.

Heifetz, R. A., Grashow, A., & Linsky, M. (2009). *The practice of adaptive leadership: Tools and tactics for changing your organization and the world*. Harvard Business Press.

Kantor, D. (2012). *Reading the room: Group dynamics for coaches and leaders*. Jossey-Bass.

Kegan, R., & Lahey, L. L. (2009). *Immunity to change: How to overcome it and unlock potential in yourself and your organization*. Harvard Business Press.

Lewis, T. H., Amini, F., & Lannon, R. (2001). *A general theory of love*. Vintage Books.

Maitlis, S. (2020). Posttraumatic growth at work. *Annual Review of Organizational Psychology and Organizational Behavior, 7*, 395–419.

Specht, D., & Tsilman, J. (2018). Teaching vicarious trauma in the journalism classroom: An examination of educational provision in UK universities. *Journal of Applied Journalism and Media Studies, 7*(2), 407–427.

Van der Kolk, B. (2014). *The body keeps the score: Brain, mind, and body in the healing of trauma*. Viking.

# Index

**A**
Adaptive leadership, 16, 71, 90, 101
Adult developmental psychology, xii
Affect, 4–6, 14–16, 19, 23, 70
Affect labeling, 66, 67, 69–71, 102
Allostatic load, 68
Alternative ways of working, 10, 51
Anxiety, 32, 43, 49, 50, 60, 68, 99
Aphasia, 36
Aprosodia, 35, 37–40
Aristotelian rhetorical appeals, 1

**B**
Behavioral science, 7, 9, 23, 24
Behavior change, xi, xiii, 30
Body politics, 48
Boyatzis, Richard, 2, 6
Brain-body integration, 33
Brand communications, 11
Broca's area, 36

**C**
Cartesian framework, 29, 31, 31
Chief Communications Officers (CCOs), 17, 18
Clusivity, 88
Cognitive distortions, 70, 71
Cognitive reframing, 66, 67, 70, 71, 100
Collaboration, xi, xiii, 10, 15, 24, 56, 63, 71, 80
Communication domains, 4, 5, 14, 15
Compassion, 94, 100, 102
Consistency theory, xiii, 57
Construct of leadership, 62
Contagion of affect, 6
Corporate social responsibility (CSR), 11, 15
Covid-19 pandemic, 10, 38, 50–52
Creativity, 36, 41, 49, 50
Cross-cultural training, xiii
Cultural dimensions, 76
Cultural neuroscience, 75–79

**D**
Damasio, Antonio, 30
Data mining, 85

© The Editor(s) (if applicable) and The Author(s), under exclusive license to Springer Nature Singapore Pte Ltd. 2022
L. McHale, *Neuroscience for Organizational Communication*,
https://doi.org/10.1007/978-981-16-7037-4

Decision-making, xii, xiii, 29, 31, 32
Default mode network (DMN), 2, 15
Descartes's error, 32
Discourse, 4, 37, 86
Disinformation, 20, 22
Dissonant leadership, 6
Diversity, 57, 61, 90
Dopamine, 63

**E**
Email, 13, 39–41, 72, 76, 93, 94, 99
Embodied cognition, 50
Embodiment, 50
Emojis, 40
Emotional processing, 29, 31, 32, 37, 38
Emotional regulation, xi, xiii, 37, 50, 68–70
Emotion centers, 31
Employee motivation, xiii
Enterprise social media platforms (ESMPs), 20
Ethos, 3–5, 94
Eudaimonic wellbeing, 63
Executive coaching, xiii
Executive functions, 6, 30
External communications, 11, 12, 16, 90

**F**
Flexible working, 10, 52
Frontal lobes, 30, 31, 44, 67

**G**
Gage, Phineas, 29–32, 37
Gender, 62, 89
Generative dialogue, ix, 15
Generative language models, 9, 11, 21–23
Goldberg, Elkhonon, 31, 36, 44, 67

GPT-3, 9, 11, 21, 22
Grawe, Klaus, 57, 58
Grieving and loss, 32, 97, 101
Groupthink, 41

**H**
Heikkilä, Melissa, 22
Hemispheric distinctions, 36
Hill, Andrew, 7
Homo economicus, 31, 32
Human needs, xiii, 49, 55, 57, 59, 61, 62, 89

**I**
Imitation game, 22
Inclusion, 14, 57, 59, 90
Inclusive and exclusive "we", 85
Innovation, 15, 24, 41
Intercultural competence, 75, 76
Intercultural competency, xiii, 56
Internal communications, 11, 12, 16, 20, 24, 60, 92
Interoception, 47, 50, 52
Intuition, xii
Investor relations, 16, 92
Invisibility, 40, 43

**J**
Journalism, 14, 18, 19, 21

**K**
Kantor, David, 1, 3–6, 14, 15, 71, 94, 101
Kellerman, Barbara, 2, 62

**L**
Latent variable, 24
Leadership communications, 78, 90, 99, 100

Leadership development, xiii, 2, 14, 56
Leadership psychology, xi, xii, xix
Logos, 3, 4, 6

**M**
Marketing, 7, 11–13, 76
Meaning, 4, 6, 14–16, 19, 23, 25, 38, 88, 91, 100, 101
Mindfulness, 33, 66–69, 71, 72
Mirror neurons, 6, 37
Modal words, 85, 91, 93, 94
Moral story, 71

**N**
Narcissism, 43, 90
Natural language processing, 92
Neurocommunicator's toolkit, 65, 67, 70, 71, 100
Neurocultural leadership, 75, 79
Neuroleadership, xii, xiii, 7, 55–57, 62, 63
Neuromania, 1, 7
Neuroplasticity, 44
Neuropsychology, 7
Neuroscience of leadership, xii, xix, 55, 56
Neuroscience of stress, 65, 66
Norepinephrine, 63

**O**
Occupational aprosodia, 35, 38–40
Office layouts, 51
Organizational change, xiii, 60
Organizational culture, xix, 2, 5, 14–17, 60, 62
Organizational growth, xiii, 56

**P**
Pathos, 3, 4, 6

Pillay, Srini, 5
Post-traumatic organizational growth, 97, 100
Power, 4, 5, 12, 14–16, 18, 19, 31, 36, 62, 67, 70, 75, 86, 94
Prefrontal cortex, 6, 7, 30, 32, 33, 63, 65, 66, 102
Prevention strategies, 12, 15
Privacy, 10, 21, 43, 93
Privilege, ix, 17, 22, 48, 89
Promotion strategies, 12, 14
Pronoun agility, 75, 79, 80
Pronoun manipulation, 78, 79
Proprioception, 47, 50, 52
Prosody, 35, 37, 38, 40, 43
Psychological safety, 3, 6, 14, 15, 58, 63, 72

**R**
Racial/cultural identity, 62, 89
Reinforcement learning systems, 22
Reward, 56, 59–61, 63, 89, 101
Reputation management, 12, 13, 16
Resonant leadership, 6
Right ventral lateral prefrontal cortex (RVLPFC), 65, 66
Rock, David, xii, xiii, 56
Role ambiguity, 12

**S**
Self-categorization theory, 41
Self-construal, 75, 77–79
Self-control, 66
Self-esteem, Control, Orientation, Attachment, and Pleasure (SCOAP) model, 55, 57–59, 61, 62, 89, 100
Self-face, 43, 44
Sensemaking, 100
Sentiment analysis, 85, 92–94
Social exclusion, 57

Social media, 3, 11, 20–22, 35, 40, 41
Somatic experience of work, 34, 47
Somatic marker hypothesis, 29, 32, 33, 50
Statistical analysis, 23–25, 62
Status, Certainty, Autonomy, Relatedness, and Fairness (SCARF™) model, 55–62, 89, 94, 100
Storytelling, 72
Stress cascade, 33, 65, 66
Structural dynamics, ix, 1, 3–6, 14, 15, 19, 70, 71, 94
Structural story, 71
Surveillance, 40, 43
Systems theory, xii, 1, 3, 14, 62, 63

**T**
Task positive network (TPN), 2, 3, 5, 15
Threat, 42, 59–61, 63, 66, 67, 94

Toxic online disinhibition, 40
Trait theory, 62
Transparency, 12, 13

**U**
Uncertainty, 41, 42, 90, 92

**V**
Vicarious traumatization, 97–99
Vulnerability, 85, 94, 98

**W**
Weasel words, 85, 91
Wernicke's area, 35, 36
Workplace redesign, 47

**Z**
Zeitgeber, 49
Zoom, 38, 42–44
Zoom fatigue, 42, 43

Printed in the United States
by Baker & Taylor Publisher Services